THE
LITTLE
BOOK
OF
BRISTOL

THE
LITTLE
BOOK
OF
BRISTOL

MAURICE FELLS

Front cover image: © Shutterstock

First published 2015
Reprinted 2017

The History Press
The Mill, Brimscombe Port
Stroud, Gloucestershire, GL5 2QG
www.thehistorypress.co.uk

British Library Cataloguing in Publication Data.
A catalogue record for this book is available from the British Library.

ISBN 978 0 7509 6195 0

Typesetting and origination by The History Press
Printed and bound in Great Britain by TJ International Ltd.

CONTENTS

Acknowledgements   7

Introduction   9

1.   What They Said About Bristol   11

2.   Welcome to Quirky Bristol   15

3.   Around the City   31

4.   Saints, Spires and Steeples   46

5.   Wartime Matters   60

6.   People Who Put Bristol on the Map   69

7.   The City at Work   77

8.   The World of Entertainment   94

9.   Literary Bristol   109

10. Transports of Delight   119

11. On the Airwaves   129

12. Law and Order   138

13. The Natural World   148

14. Sporting Bristol   156

15. On This Day   170

About the Author   188

ACKNOWLEDGEMENTS

As a passionate born and bred Bristolian, the research and writing of this book has been a labour of love. To pull all the information for this book together, I started by trawling through my own archive of press releases, house magazines and other publicity material issued by old established firms long ago. Many of these firms no longer exist, while others have been swallowed up by global conglomerates.

Reading some of Bristol's long-extinct newspapers also proved to be a rich source of information. The *Western Daily Press,* from its first edition in the middle of the nineteenth century to the present day, was extremely useful, as was the *Bristol Evening Post* founded in 1932.

The staff at Bristol Central Library were, as ever, most patient and extremely helpful in dealing with my numerous enquiries.

I must thank Jan and Simon Fuller for access to their collection of Bristol memorabilia from old theatre programmes to newspaper cuttings.

My thanks also go to Nicola Guy at The History Press for asking me if I would like to write this book.

Last, but certainly not least, I owe a special debt of gratitude to Janet and Trevor Naylor. This is not only for their flow of most helpful advice and suggestions but also for their constant encouragement without which I know this book may never have been completed.

Maurice Fells, 2015

INTRODUCTION

There can't be many cities where you'll find a sofa on the street corner, or a university housed in a bungalow, or even where the Lord Mayor runs in a half-marathon wearing his full civic regalia of tricorn hat, red robes and chain of office.

This is Bristol, a city that dates back more than 1,000 years but not one that is sleeping in the shadows of its ancient past. It is a successful, modern city, effectively the capital of the West of England.

The city traditionally prospered from the vices of the wine, tobacco and slave trades, but in their stead Bristol has become a thriving financial and new media centre. But that's not to say it's full of pinstripe-suited accountants and keyboard tappers, for it also has its bohemian quarter, as well as its cultural and sporting side. It was the birthplace of the graffiti artist Banksy and the trip-hop genre of music.

Wine may not play such an important role in the city's economy as it did for many years but Bristol can boast having the biggest wine warehouse in Europe. It can, would you believe, hold 57 million bottles of wine at one time.

It is fascinating, but maybe frivolous, and sometimes bizarre facts like this that you will find in this book, which does not pretend to be a definitive or chronological history of Bristol. It is simply a compendium of interesting facts from both the past and the present which I hope will interest visitors or newcomers to the city alike as well as those born and bred here who thought they really knew their city.

1

WHAT THEY SAID ABOUT BRISTOL

On a visit to Bristol, the twelfth-century chronicler William of Malmesbury described the port as being 'full of ships from Ireland, Norway and every part of Europe, which brought hither great commerce and much foreign wealth'.

King Henry VII found the women of Bristol to be so 'sumptuously apparelled' that he ordered every man worth £20 in goods to pay him £1.

It seems that on a week-long visit to Bristol in 1574, Queen Elizabeth was not impressed by the city's women as she said: 'By the bones of my father, Mr Mayor, but I protest I never saw so ugly a collection of women as your city can assemble.'

The opinion most commonly known about St Mary Redcliffe church is the one reputed to have been uttered by Elizabeth I on her visit to the city in 1574. She is said to have described it as 'The fairest, goodliest and most famous parish church in England'. However, no record of her saying this has ever been found. If she didn't say it, she should have.

Just over a century later, Charles I said something similar about St Mary Redcliffe. He declared: 'The parish church of Redcliffe for the foundation structures and buildings thereof is one of the most famous absolute fairest and goodliest parish churches within the realm of England.'

On a visit to Bristol, William Camden, a sixteenth-century chronicler, noted: 'There is a church called Temple, whose tower shakes when the bells ring, that it has parted from the rest of the building, and left a chink from top to bottom three fingers abroad, opening and closing as the bells ring.'

The queen of James I visited the city in 1613 and was entertained with a sham sea-fight and other events. Thanking the city, Her Majesty is reported to have said that 'I never knew I was Queen until I came to Bristol'.

'In this city are many proper men, but very few handsome women, and most of them ill bred, being generally men and women very proud, not affable to strangers, but rather much admiring themselves.' Marmaduke Rawdon, a merchant from York, said on a visit to Bristol in the seventeenth century.

Diarist John Evelyn, who visited Bristol in 1654, said that the city was 'emulating London in its manner of building, its shops and bridge'.

'In every respect another London that one can hardly know it to stand in the country,' said Samuel Pepys, diarist, on a visit to the city in 1668. He went on to say that his host provided 'good entertainment of strawberries, a whole venison, pasty and plenty of brave wine and above all Bristol Milk'.

The poet and satirist Alexander Pope, writing about the docks in 1739, said: 'In the middle of the street, as far as you can see, hundreds of ships, their masts as thick as they can stand by one another, which is the oddest and most surprising sight imaginable. The street is fuller of them than the Thames from London Bridge to Deptford.'

William Cobbett (1763–1835), farmer, politician and writer who travelled around southern England on horseback, said that Bristol was 'a good and solid and wealthy city and people of plain and good manners, private virtue and public spirit united … as to the seat of the city and its environs, it surpasses all I ever saw'. Cobbett also wrote: 'A great commercial city in the midst of cornfields, meadows and woods.'

Besides writing the popular novel *Robinson Crusoe,* Daniel Defoe was the author of many other books, including *Tour Through the Whole Island of Great Britain* in which he said of Bristol: 'The greatest, the richest and the best port of trade in Great Britain, London only excepted.' He also said: 'There are no less than fifteen glass houses in Bristol which is more than there are in the city of London; they have indeed a very great experience of glass bottles, sending them fill'd with beer, cyder and wine to the West Indies, much more than goes to London.'

Horace Walpole, English art historian, man of letters and politician, was rather damning about the city. In 1776 he wrote: 'I did go to Bristol, the dirtiest great shop I ever saw, with so foul a river that had I seen the least appearance of cleanliness I should have concluded they washed all their linen in it.'

Bristol-born Robert Southey, who was Poet Laureate from 1813 until his death thirty years later, wrote: 'The beautiful vale of Ashton is the place of all others which I remember with most feeling.' He may have been biased for some of his relatives are buried in the churchyard at Long Ashton.

In 1799 Lady Hesketh, who is buried in Bristol Cathedral, wrote: 'The Bristol people have done all in their power to ruin the rural beauties of Clifton Hill by the number of abominable buildings they have erected all over it … but it is always preferable to any other place.'

'Everyone stays at home and one never sees a fashionable man in the street' – Eugenie Montijo, later to become Empress of France, speaking about her time in Clifton when she was sent to a finishing school on Royal York Crescent in 1837.

Travel writer H.V. Morton, in his book *In Search of England*, published in 1927, said: 'Nothing to see in Bristol! There is too much to see there! I could stay for a month and write you a different story every day.' He went on: 'My trouble in Bristol is that I cannot leave the byways. It is a city as fascinating as London; and in the same unselfconscious way.' He also wrote: 'Ships come right into Bristol town … and the men of Bristol think nothing of it. They have been accustomed to this disturbing sight for over nine centuries.'

The Victorian engineer Isambard Kingdom Brunel, who did so much to change the face of Bristol, said that the people who backed his many projects were 'The spirited merchants of Bristol'.

In her novel *Evelina,* the writer and diarist Fanny Burney (1752–1840) has her heroine saying of Hotwells: 'A most delightful spot; the prospect is beautiful, the air pure and the water very favourable to invalids.'

J.B. Priestly, writer and broadcaster, wrote in 1933: 'What is admirable about Bristol is that it is both old and alive, and not one of your museum pieces, living on tourists and the sale of bogus antiques.'

Poet Laureate Sir John Betjeman states: 'Bristol is the most beautiful, interesting and distinguished city in England.' He also said: 'Bristol's biggest surprise is Clifton, a sort of Bath consisting of Regency crescents and terraces overlooking the Avon Gorge to the blue hills of Somerset' and …

'There is no city in England with so much charm.'

'The hotel would be a monster and utterly unsuitable for the site. The Avon Gorge is a natural piece of unique scenery' – Sir John Betjeman, speaking at a public inquiry in Bristol in 1971 about plans for a multi-storey hotel to be built on the rock face next to the Clifton Suspension Bridge. After studying the inspector's report the then Environment Minister, Peter Walker, rejected the proposals for a hotel.

A *Sunday Times* survey published in 2014 said that the best city in the country to live in was Bristol. The paper told its readers: 'It offers bucket-loads of history and heritage from Brunel to Banksy, along with a great choice of housing, fantastic transport links (which are set to get even better following a rail upgrade in 2017 that will see journey times to London cut to eighty minutes) and a real sense of growing economic importance and creative energy.'

2

WELCOME TO QUIRKY BRISTOL

SOFAS ON THE STREET CORNERS

Bristol was the first place in the United Kingdom to ban traffic from its city-centre streets on the first Sunday of each summer month to turn them into a playground for families. The traffic-free streets became packed with food stalls, stilt walkers, jugglers, dancers, musicians and the like. Sofas were even provided for people to slump in. It is all part of a 'Make Sunday Special' scheme introduced by the Mayor of Bristol.

In May 2014, nearly 100,000 people signed up for the chance to get a free 'ticket to slide', sliding down a 300ft-long water chute that had been specially installed on Park Street in the centre of the city for a 'Make Sunday Special' event. Some of those wanting to traverse the chute on a lilo lived in Abu Dhabi but were prepared to fly to Bristol for an experience that lasted less than thirty seconds. In the event only 360 people were lucky enough to get a ticket through a ballot.

GOING IT ALONE

You won't find the Peoples' Republic of Stokes Croft on any map or listed in any street directory by that description. This bohemian inner-city area of Stokes Croft was given that name by community activists in 2007 – and it has stuck ever since – to promote the city's alternative cultural quarter with its independent shops, workers' co-ops and extensive street art.

Bristol was one of the eleven largest cities in England to hold a referendum in 2012 to discover whether or not the electorate wanted a Directly Elected Mayor. The holder of this new office would provide political leadership and replace the existing council leaders. In the event, Bristol was the only city to vote in favour of having a mayor. In the referendum 41,032 people ticked the 'Yes' box on their ballot paper while 35,880 were against. Later the same year fifteen candidates stood in the election for a Directly Elected Mayor. George Ferguson, an architect known for his trademark red trousers, who stood as an independent candidate, won the poll with 37,353 votes. The Labour Party candidate came second with 31,259 votes. There was a turnout of 28 per cent of the electorate.

ANIMAL TRAILS

Sixty-one multi-coloured, life-size, fibreglass gorillas were installed on the streets and parks of Bristol in the summer of 2011 and people were challenged to track them all down. The gorilla trail was organised by Bristol Zoo to mark its 175th anniversary. The sculptures were later sold at an auction, which raised £427,000 for gorilla conservation work and the Bristol Royal Hospital for Children.

Eighty brightly painted sculptures of Gromit the dog created by Aardman Animation Films of Bristol took over the city's streets during the summer of 2013 for the Gromit Unleashed trail. These sculptures also went under the auctioneer's hammer and raised £2.3 million for the Children's Hospital.

Giant individually designed sculptures of Shaun the Sheep, a creation of Aardman Films, took to the streets and parks of Bristol and London in the summer of 2015. The sixty sculptures in each city were decorated by celebrities and artists to raise funds for sick children. Shaun was voted the nation's all-time favourite BBC children's television character in 2014.

RETAIL THERAPY

Gloucester Road, part of the A38 running through north Bristol, has the largest number of independent traders, from fashion emporiums to grocers and from record shops to ironmongers, on any one road in the United Kingdom.

St Nicholas covered market in Bristol's 'Old Quarter' is the oldest market in the city. It dates back to 1743 and has the largest collection of independent traders under one roof in Bristol.

The fifteenth-century Christmas Steps, which rises from Host Street to Colston Street, must be the city's quirkiest shopping area. Small independently run shops line each side of the forty-nine steps, selling everything from handmade shoes to fish and chips.

KEEPING IT CLEAN

A Bristol Corporation deed of 1533 ratified the right of washerwomen to dry their clothing and linen by stretching it across the bushes on Brandon Hill Park. Carpet beating was also allowed on the park but only during certain hours.

MAYORAL MOMENTS

Robert Ricart, who was Town Clerk in the fifteenth century, recorded in his 'Maire's Kalendar' that one of his duties was to provide dice for the mayor and councillors when they were killing time waiting for people to arrive.

Alderman Thomas Proctor, who built a twenty-one-room mansion on the edge of Clifton Downs for himself and his wife, later gave it away to the city council in 1874. His unusual gift included fixtures and fittings along with a £500 cheque for repairs and decorations. Since then Mr Proctor's former home has been known as the Mansion House. It has become the official residence and office of the Lord Mayor during his or her year of office. Bristol is one of the few cities outside London that has a Mansion House for its leading citizen.

Bristol has had a mayor since 1216 and a Lord Mayor since 1899 following an announcement by Queen Victoria on her birthday that the city should have this honour. The queen also granted the Lord Mayor the right to be styled as 'the Right Honourable'.

Instead of knighting Councillor Herbert Ashman, the first Lord Mayor of Bristol, at Buckingham Palace, Queen Victoria bestowed the honour on him in 1899 outside the Council House then in Corn Street. Her Majesty dubbed Mr Ashman on the shoulder with a borrowed sword – without even leaving her horse-drawn landau.

When he was mayor, Councillor William Proctor Baker proved he had a head for heights by laying the capstone of the spire of St Mary Redcliffe church, which was nearly 300ft above street level. He was hoisted part of the way up the spire in a makeshift lift made of boards, ropes and cloth and climbed the rest. He then tapped the 1-ton capstone into place, which was the final act of the restoration of St Mary Redcliffe in 1872. Part of the church's spire had crashed across the nave during a violent thunder and lightning storm 426 years earlier.

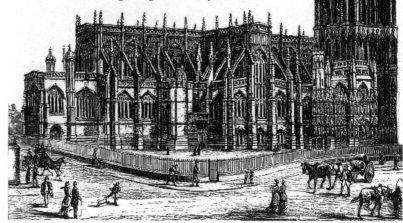

During his term of office as Lord Mayor in 2012, Councillor Peter Main helped celebrate the fortieth anniversary of Dean Field Studies Centre, which is run by the city council. Apart from unveiling the obligatory plaque, Mr Main in his full mayoral robes took a quick trip down a zip wire. However, he had to swap his ceremonial feathered tricorn hat for a hard helmet for safety reasons.

WANT TO GET AHEAD? WEAR A HAT

The City Swordbearer, who precedes the Lord Mayor in procession, is the only person whose head can be covered in the presence of royalty. This is because the sword is so heavy it needs two hands to carry it. The Swordbearer's role dates back to 1373 and the headgear from Elizabethan times. It is formally known as the Cap of Maintenance – a furry Cossack-style affair – which wouldn't look out of place in a Gilbert and Sullivan opera.

THE TAXPAYER'S CHURCH

St Mark's chapel, better known as the Lord Mayor's chapel, is the only place of worship in England owned and maintained by a local authority, or perhaps more accurately the council taxpayers. Bristol Corporation bought the chapel on College Green in 1541 for £1,000 from Henry VIII. However, councillors continued to worship at Bristol Cathedral until 1722 when they fell out with the Dean and Chapter. They then decided to use St Mark's; after all they owned it. The mayor and councillors still worship at the chapel on special occasions.

THE WORLD'S SMALLEST UNIVERSITY

What can easily claim to be the smallest university in the country, if not the world, is housed in a bungalow on the large disadvantaged Withywood estate, in south Bristol. Since retired teacher Anton Bantock opened the University of Withywood in 1987 many hundreds of people have attended lectures at his home given by visiting speakers on a variety of subjects. This seat of learning also organises walks, exhibitions and musical performances for its students. The university, which is recognised as a registered charity, even has its own motto: *Ad Altiora Per Collegium Withywoodiense*, which translates as 'To higher things through Withywood'.

BRISTOL SAYINGS

'All shipshape and Bristol Fashion' means that everything has been stowed and the ship is ready to go to sea. It derives from the Port of Bristol's reputation for efficiency in the days of sail.

'Pay on the Nail' originates from the four brass pillars, or Bristol Nails, that have stood outside the Exchange in Corn Street since the sixteenth century. It was on these pillars that merchants settled their business deals with one another. A raised rim around the edge of each one prevents coins from rolling off and dropping on to the pavement.

'Happy as a sand boy' originated from the Ostrich Inn at Bathurst Basin, according to an advertising card for the pub which dates back to 1745. Boys were employed to collect sand that was shipped into the nearby docks to cover the floors of the bar. They were rewarded with jugs of ale, so hence the old saying.

A visitor to the city could be forgiven for wanting an interpreter to translate the Bristol dialect. Some of the phrases commonly used by Bristolians include:

'Where's that to?' – Where is it?

'Gert lush' – Very good.

'Ark at ee' – Look at him.

'Cheers drive' – Thanks driver. A term normally used by passengers when getting off a bus.

'Bemmie' – This is a shortened form of Bedminster, a suburb in south Bristol.

'Alright my luvver?' – How are you?

'Ow bist?' – How are you?

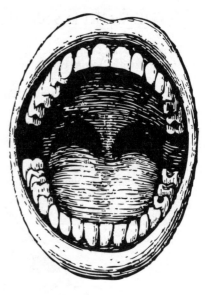

HIGH FLIERS

If you see a 'dog' floating skywards don't be alarmed. The 'dog' will be a specially shaped hot-air balloon taking part in the International Balloon Fiesta at Ashton Court. More than 120 hot-air balloons of all shape and sizes, from a house to the FA Cup, lift off in a series of mass ascents during the event each August. The fiesta – the largest of its kind in Europe – attracts balloonists from all over the world and half a million spectators. Balloon maker Don Cameron and some friends started the fiesta in 1979 with just twenty-seven balloonists taking part and it's been running every year since.

'BRITAIN'S UGLIEST POP GROUP'

The Rolling Stones may well have been the latest pop music sensation in the summer of 1964 but the staff at the Grand Hotel, Broad Street, were certainly not impressed. The tail-coated head waiter in the hotel's dining room refused to serve the rock group because they were wearing sweatshirts and jeans instead of jackets and ties. The Rolling Stones, who were playing at a concert in the nearby Colston Hall, took their custom to a nearby curry house. The incident made the front pages of the national newspapers, with the *Daily Express* describing the 'Stones' as the 'ugliest group in Britain'.

A CURE FOR ALL ILLS?

A newspaper announcement in 1799 stated that the grandly named Pneumatic Institution run by Dr Thomas Beddoes had opened in Dowry Square, Hotwells. It was here that Dr Beddoes experimented with the idea that gases produced from both ends of a cow might cure tuberculosis. The newspaper also claimed that the Institution could treat 'incurable diseases including consumption, dropsy and obstinate venereal complaints'. Beddoes employed a young Humphrey (later Sir) Davy who discovered the anaesthetic properties of nitrous oxide or laughing gas. He used the gas as a recreational drug with his newfound friends the poets Coleridge and Southey.

WALKING BY WATER

Perhaps one of the quirkiest events in the Bristol calendar is the St Mary Redcliffe Pipe Walk, which sees the vicar and his parishioners picking their way around allotments, trekking though pastureland and even peering down manholes. They are following the route of a water supply that Lord Robert de Berkeley, Lord of the Manor of Bedminster, gave to Redcliffe parish in 1190. The water flowed from a hilltop spring at Knowle to the church, a distance of just over 2 miles. The walk commemorates Lord Robert's gift and enables the church to lay claim to certain endowments. It's up to the vicar to check that the pipe is still there, hence the lifting of manhole covers.

A ROAD THAT DOES NOT OFFICIALLY EXIST

Generations of Bristolians have referred to the top of Whiteladies Road as Blackboy Hill yet it has never been listed as such in well-respected street directories, guides or maps. You won't find any Blackboy Hill street nameplates, either. Nor is it an official postal address. The name probably came from the Blackboy Inn that once straddled the top of Whiteladies Road before being demolished in 1874 for road widening. Another pub in the area changed its name in 1988 to perpetuate the Blackboy name. Whiteladies Road recalls a small thatched pub of that name which some time ago stood near the junction of Oakfield Road.

SOME UNUSUAL TALES OF ROYALTY

After being defeated at the Battle of Worcester in 1651, the future King Charles II tried to escape the Roundhead soldiers and headed west. He stayed at Leigh Court at Abbots Leigh near Bristol, the home of George Norton, disguised as a servant. Although the butler recognised the prince he passed him off as the kitchen boy. After leaving Leigh Court the prince made his way to Dorset and then on to France. When he ascended to the throne Charles II thanked George Norton for his hospitality by making him a knight.

One of the strangest requests ever received by the 'city fathers' came from the king in September 1664. He asked for 1,500 pairs of shoes and stockings to clothe his army. To fund this request it was decided that a weekly levy already imposed on householders for maintaining the garrison should be doubled for a month.

Protocol was fearlessly flouted by a boy at Clifton College who asked for the autograph of Queen Victoria's daughter, Princess Louise. A courtier from the royal household replied to his request: 'Dear Master Allen, Members of the Royal Family do not give their autographs to strangers. However, HRH Prince Louise has kindly made an exception in your favour. You are urged not to tell your school fellows the Princess has given it you, or I may receive other applications which I should only be obliged to refuse.'

The first royal visit to Clifton College must have been something of an embarrassment for all concerned. Prince Albert Victor, second in line to the throne, was in Bristol to unveil a statute of his grandmother, Queen Victoria, on College Green. He had been persuaded to pass by the college and meet some of the staff at the gates. In the event it rained and the prince arrived late. He moved on after hearing only the start of a formal welcome being read to him.

A HIDDEN ROYAL MEMORIAL

What is believed to be the only public memorial to Princess Charlotte of Wales and Saxe Coburg is virtually hidden away in the grounds of a former convalescent hospital at Redland. It takes the form of an obelisk and was commissioned by a local businessman, though it's not known why. The princess, who died aged 21 when giving birth to a stillborn son in 1817, is buried in St George's chapel, Windsor.

BRISTOL'S OWN LEANING TOWER

Bristol's answer to the leaning tower of Pisa was almost demolished in the Second World War – not by bombs but by concerned soldiers. They were unaware that the 114ft-high tower of Temple church in Victoria Street had been leaning at a precarious angle – almost 5ft out of true – since the fourteenth century. Fearing that a bomb had caused the tower to lean and further serious damage might be caused, members of the Royal Engineers wanted to pull it down. However, the entreaties of local people stopped them and saved the landmark from demolition. The church was built by the Knights Templar in the twelfth century on marshy land which probably accounts for its leaning tower.

BUILDING CURIOSITIES

It seems that the builders of Royal York Crescent in Clifton were superstitious. They did not include a number thirteen in the crescent of forty-six houses. Instead they built a 12a. Work on the crescent started in 1750 but the bankruptcy of the developer brought it to a stop. The government bought the ground and unfinished section of the crescent, intending to build barracks. Local opposition frustrated this plan and the crescent was completed in 1820 as originally envisaged.

The Black Castle at Brislington is a sham castle built in 1764 that is now a public house that even has a chapel in one of its turrets. It was originally offices and stables built for William Reeves with black slag from his foundry. On a visit to Bristol in 1766 the writer Horace Walpole described the Black Castle as a 'large Gothic building, coal black and striped with white. I took it for the Devil's Cathedral'.

Bristol City Council's administrative headquarters, known as the Council House until November 2012 but since then as City Hall, took longer to build than the Parthenon. The foundation stone was laid in June 1938 but the Second World War interrupted the work. It was not until April 1956 that the curved building was officially opened by the queen.

The gilded unicorns that stand at each end of the roof of City Hall took council officers by surprise when they were installed, for no one knew who had ordered them and the unicorns did not appear in the list of building specifications. When the architect returned from holiday he explained that the unicorns cost £2,400 whereas ornamental ridging along the length of the roof would have cost £600 more.

Prefabricated homes, which were built as a short-term fix for a post-war housing shortage, were only meant to last ten years at the most. However, as fifteen sites around Bristol testify, they were still being lived in sixty years later. Their end came when the city council completed a ten-year replacement scheme in 2014. The prefabs were built by the Bristol Aeroplane Company from aluminium that had been salvaged from crashed aircraft. A prefab at Shirehampton was the first to be completed and occupied in 1945.

THREE COLOURFUL CHARACTERS

George Pocock, who ran his own school – Prospect Place Academy in Kingsdown – in the nineteenth century, invented what he called a 'thrashing machine' for chastising errant pupils. His contraption consisted of a rotating wheel with artificial hands that was able to administer 'six of the best' to any schoolboy that offended. It meant that Pocock didn't have to physically exert himself.

Self-styled 'professor' Charlie Stephens was a barber and stuntman who loved tempting fate. He did such things as shaving customers in a lion's cage and balancing an apple on his throat so it could be split in two by a sword. Stephens, who was known as the 'demon barber of Bedminster' attempted to go over the Niagara Falls in 1920 in a custom-built barrel. It was made from 2in-thick Russian oak and equipped with an oxygen tank and breathing mask. But all of Stephens' plans were to no avail for he lost his life in his madcap stunt.

At least one vicar was discovered in the eighteenth century to be sup-plementing his income by running a pub. The Revd Emanuel Collins, who kept the Duke of Marlborough in Bedminster, boosted his sti-pend by charging fees to conduct illegal marriages at the bar. The pub was later advertised for sale.

DRINKING FOR A RECORD

The Old Duke in King Street was packed with about 800 students coming and going one night in March 1965. They were aiming to beat their own world record of drinking a pub dry. However, only 1,000 pints went down the 'hatch' compared with the 2,450 the students consumed the previous year.

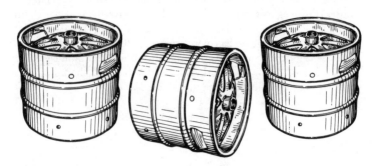

WIFE FOR SALE

When the new Cattle Market near Temple Meads railway station opened in 1830 it was announced that there was space for 7,000 sheep, 5,000 pigs, 300 horses, five compartments for fat beasts holding 50 each, and ten for lean beasts holding 80 each. But one of the first 'lots' to go under the auctioneer's hammer was the wife of a man from Felton. The highest price the auctioneer could get for the lady was £5 10s.

BONFIRE NIGHT BELLS

Ringers at St Luke's church, Brislington, used to be paid 5s to ring the tower bells to celebrate the failure of the gunpowder plot.

A TOUCH OF VENICE

The former Lloyds Bank branch in Corn Street was built between 1854 and 1857 in an opulent Venetian style, copying St Mark's Library in Venice. A frieze on the facade has cherubs depicting the activities of the bank, which include receiving, paying, storing, coining money, engraving and printing, and trading with Africa and America.

Brown's restaurant in Clifton is modelled on the Doge's Palace in Venice. The building was once part of the Bristol Museum and Art Gallery.

... AND A HINT OF ROME?

And finally ... Bristol, like Rome, is built on seven hills – but that's the only thing the two cities have in common.

3

AROUND
THE CITY

THE TEN TALLEST BUILDINGS

St Mary Redcliffe church, Redcliffe Way
With its elegant and stately spire soaring 292ft above street level, this is the tallest building in the city.

Castlemead, Lower Castle Street
This eighteen-storey office block, completed in 1964, is 262ft high.

Wills Memorial Building, Clifton
This neo-Gothic tower, which is part of Bristol University's campus, rises 215ft from street level.

Christ Church, Clifton
The capstone of the church's spire is 215ft above the ground.

Eclipse, Cabot Circus
This is a thirteen-storey block of apartments 213ft high, built on the edge of the Cabot Circus shopping and leisure development.

Colston Tower, Colston Avenue
This fifteen-storey office block is 207ft high.

Froomsgate House, Rupert Street
This is another fifteen-storey office block, also 207ft high.

Premier Inn, The Haymarket
Overlooking one of Bristol's busiest traffic roundabouts, this 200ft-high building was originally the administrative headquarters of Avon County Council from its inception in 1973 until 1996 when the authority was abolished. It has since been converted into a hotel.

One Redcliffe Street, Redcliffe
This fifteen-storey 200ft-high building beside Bristol Bridge was the first skyscraper office block in the city. It was built in 1963 as headquarters for the E.S. and A. Robinson printing and packaging group. It did not meet with everyone's approval, though. Architectural students from Bristol University called for its demolition, claiming it was 'ugly'. To underline their case the students set fire to a cardboard model of the £1 million block. The building is now occupied by various firms.

Clifton Heights, The Triangle, Clifton
This 160ft-high block was something of a white elephant when it was built in 1964, with street-level showrooms, two floors of offices above and forty-eight apartments on top of that. Only three apartments were ever occupied and one of those was by the building's caretaker. Clifton Heights has since been revamped with bars and restaurants on the ground floor whilst the flats have been converted into offices.

FOUR HIGH SPOTS

The top of the spire of Christ Church, Clifton, is 477ft above sea level.

Observatory Hill, once an Iron Age camp, beside Clifton Suspension Bridge, is 338ft above the high-water mark of the River Avon.

Brandon Hill Park, off Park Street, rises to 250ft at its highest point. Cabot Tower, a memorial to the explorer John Cabot, which itself is 105ft high, stands on the park's highest point.

The road of the Clifton Suspension Bridge is 245ft above high water.

BUILDINGS OF SPECIAL INTEREST

A house in Church Road, Westbury-on-Trym, is reputed to be the oldest domestic building in the city. This was the home of Elsie Briggs from 1958 until her death in 1988. She left the house, which dates back to the fifteenth century, to trustees who are charged with keeping it as an ecumenical place of contemplative prayer. It is now named after Elsie Briggs.

There are nearly 4,500 buildings in the city on the United Kingdom's register of places of special architectural merit and/or heritage. One hundred of them are Grade I, 500 are Grade II* and the rest are Grade II.

Ten Grade I buildings, installations or structures
Bristol Cathedral; the Central Library; Theatre Royal; Temple Meads railway station; the equestrian statue of King William III in Queen Square; Clifton Suspension Bridge; St Mary Redcliffe church; Kings Weston House and the Holy Trinity church, Westbury-on-Trym.

Ten Grade II* buildings and structures
The entrance lodge and gates of Arnos Vale cemetery; numbers 2–9 Albemarle Row, Hotwells; Bishopsworth Manor, a privately owned house at Bishopsworth; the Clifton Club; City Hall; the Victoria public house, Clifton; Clifton Lido; Blaise Castle; Clifton Cathedral and Bristol Cathedral School.

MEASURING UP THE CITY

Bristol under water

There are 47 square miles of Bristol under water as opposed to 43 above. This is because the city's sea boundaries reach down to the islands of Steep Holm and Flat Holm in the Bristol Channel, which lie between Cardiff and Weston-super-Mare. The sea boundary skirts around Clevedon Pier and includes the lighthouse on Battery Point at Portishead. It then returns to dry land via tiny Denny Island heading for Avonmouth, from where the river boundary goes to Chittening Warth, north of Avonmouth, under Clifton Suspension Bridge and on to its most northerly point at Hanham Weir.

Beating the Bounds

For many years the mayor and council officials took part in a ceremony known as Beating the Bounds. This was an ancient custom of inspecting the boundaries of a parish or town. In Bristol's case this involved a four-day trek on the land and a trip by steamboat on the fifth day to the islands of Steep Holm and Flat Holm. Those taking part for the first time were bumped on marker stones along the route. By about 1900 the ceremony had become such a popular event that a group of young women formed a volunteer 'bumping corps' and dealt vigorously with many of the walkers.

GREEN CITY

Bristol has more than 450 green spaces ranging from Clifton and Durdham Downs of 450 acres to Queen Square of 2.9 acres. Although the city council owns Ashton Court estate and its mansion, totalling 840 acres, most of the site lies in north Somerset. The council bought it in 1960 for £103,200. It had been in the ownership of the Smyth family for four centuries.

College Green, with Bristol Cathedral on one side and City Hall overlooking it, is an open space of 2.7 acres. It takes the shape of a segment of a circle and was once a burial ground. College Green is owned by the Dean and Chapter of Bristol Cathedral but maintained by the city council.

The city was awarded the title of European Green Capital 2015 by the European Commission. It was chosen from three other finalists – Brussels, Glasgow and Ljubljana, the capital of Slovenia. The title recognises Bristol's environmental achievements, its future commitments and its ability to inspire others. Bristol is the first UK city to hold the title.

COUNTING HEADS

At the time of Domesday Book in 1886 the city's population was estimated to be 2,300. By the time of the Poll Tax returns of 1377 its population had trebled to more than 6,000. According to the latest figures available from the 2011 census Bristol's population is 432,000 with nearly another 4 million people living within an hour's drive of the city.

Strangely, Bristol didn't even get a mention of its own in Domesday Book although what is now the suburb of Clifton did. Clifton, then a hamlet, had a population of just thirty people, comprising 'villeins' (tenant farmers) 'bords' (poultry farmers) and 'serfs' (unpaid workers). Domesday Book showed Bristol as part of the Manor of Barton. The name Barton survives in the suburb of Barton Hill.

James Sketchley produced the first Bristol Directory in 1775. It was a long alphabetical list of the names and addresses of the merchants and tradesmen, although a few private residents had their names included. Amongst the merchants were whip makers and muffin makers. Sketchley estimated the population of Bristol in 1775 as 35,440.

ROYAL CHARTERS

Bristol was granted its first royal charter in 1155. This gave toll-free passages through England, Wales and Normandy for all merchants.

A charter granted in 1373 by Edward III made Bristol a county in its own right. It was the first borough in the country to be awarded such status. Until then Bristol was in Gloucestershire, but the charter made it a county that was separated from Gloucestershire to the north and Somerset to the south. Bristol had paid the king 600 marks for the charter, which became known as Bristol's Magna Carta. In granting it the king was also showing his appreciation to the town, which provided him with ships and men for the wars in France.

To mark the granting of the charter, Bristol commissioned the building of what became known as the High Cross. This was a monument 39ft 6in high with niches that were gradually filled with statues of monarchs that granted the county with further charters.

The High Cross, which became an assembly point for civic processions and a place where the mayor made proclamations, originally stood at the junction of Broad Street, High Street, Corn Street and Wine Street, then the centre of the town. It was later moved to College Green. However, in 1764 Bristol lost the cross forever. Dean Cutts Barton, the Dean of Bristol, gave it away to his friend Henry Hoare of Stourhead Park, Wiltshire, and it's stood there ever since. However, the remains of a replica of the High Cross stand in Berkeley Square, Clifton.

In 1542 Henry VIII conferred on Bristol the status of a city. It meant that Bristol then became a city and a county in its own right.

BRISTOL BY TRADITION

A stonemason is called in by the council after each new Lord Mayor is appointed so that his or her name can be engraved on a wall of civic fame in City Hall. The list of mayors and Lord Mayors dates back to 1216.

The Freedom of Bristol is the highest honour that the city council can grant. It is normally awarded to individuals who have 'given distinguished and eminent service' to the city. However, it has also been conferred on Hannover, one of Bristol's 'twin cities', the warship HMS *Bristol*, and the Bristol district branch of the Merchant Navy Association. The Gloucestershire Regiment – now the Rifles Regiment – has been granted the Freedom twice. On both occasions the 'Glorious Glosters', as they are known, exercised their right to march through the city with bayonets fixed, drums beating and regimental flags flying.

Bristol is one of the few cities in the country to have Lord Mayor's Trumpeters. The two trumpeters wear ceremonial dress of blue coats and breeches, waistcoats and black velvet caps. They herald the arrival of the queen with a fanfare when she visits Bristol and also the Lord Mayor at major civic occasions. Their role dates back to the seventeenth century.

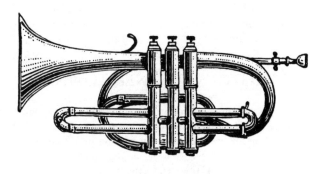

SELLING THE 'FAMILY SILVER'

To raise much-needed funds, the council in 1836 auctioned 520 dozen bottles of wine in its cellars for a profit of £500. This included the choicest port, sherry and Old East India Madeira. A few days later furniture from the Mansion House fetched £725 at another auction.

LANGUAGES SPOKEN IN BRISTOL

Being a large cosmopolitan city, many different languages can now be heard in Bristol. They include:

Albanian	Lingala
Amharic	Lithuanian
Arabic	Pashto
Bengali	Persian
Bulgarian	Polish
Chinese, Cantonese and Mandarin	Portuguese
Czech	Punjabi
Dari (Farsi, Persian)	Romanian
Eritrean	Russian
French	Slovak
German	Somali
Greek	Spanish
Gujarati	Swahili
Hindi	Sylheti
Hungarian	Tamil
Italian	Thai
Japanese	Tigrinya
Korean	Turkish
Kurdish	Ukranian
Kurdish Badin and Sorani	Urdu
Kurmanji	Vietnamese

BRISTOL'S TWINNED TOWNS

Bristol has been twinned with Bordeaux, France, running family-to-family exchanges for students at secondary schools since 1947. Since then it has set up further twinned town relationships with:

Hannover, Germany
Oporto, Portugal
Tbilisi, Georgia
Puerto Morazan, Nicaragua
Beira, Mozambique
Guangzhai, China

WHAT'S IN A NAME?

Some Bristolians like to think America takes its name from Richard Amerike who lived at Long Ashton. As the Collector of Customs he had the responsibility of paying a pension to the explorer John Cabot on behalf of the king. Cabot had sailed from Bristol in 1497 in search of spices from the East but made landfall at Newfoundland. Records show that Amerike made several payments to Cabot on behalf of Henry VII.

Bristol has many namesakes in the world. Most of them are villages, towns and cities in the United States. They are located in:

Colorado	Maryland	Rhode Island
Connecticut	Michigan	South Dakota
Florida	Minnesota	Tennessee
Georgia	Missouri	Texas
Illinois	Nevada	Vermont
Indiana	New Hampshire	Virginia
Iowa	New York	Washington
Louisiana	Ohio	West Virginia
Maine	Pennsylvania	Wisconsin

Other places in the world named Bristol:

There is an arm of the Bering Sea called Bristol Bay

There is also a borough called Bristol Bay in South West Alaska

Bristol Channel is an inlet of the Atlantic Ocean
separating Wales from south-west England

Bristol Ferry is a hamlet at the north end of Rhode Island, America

Bristol Lake is an intermittently dry bed in California

Bristol Island is part of the South Sandwich
Islands in the southern Atlantic Ocean

Bristol Mountains can be found in the Mojave
Desert, California, America

There is a village called Bristol in New Brunswick and a municipality
known by the same name in Quebec, both in Canada

HOTEL BRISTOL

There are more than 200 hotels around the world called Bristol but none of them are named after the English city. All take their name from Frederick Hervey, 4th Earl of Bristol and Bishop of Derry. He was widely travelled, especially around Europe, and had a reputation for only staying at the best hotels. Hence those he visited changed their names to Hotel Bristol. The title of Marquis of Bristol has been held by a member of the Hervey family since 1714.

SEVEN HISTORIC PUBS

A pub has stood on the site of the **Rummer Inn**, All Saints Lane, since 1246 when it was known as the Green Lattice after its exterior decorations. In 1965 it became the first Berni steak and chips restaurant in the country. Its owners, the Bristol-based Italian brothers Frank and Aldo Berni, went on to build up a chain of more than 140 similar pubs that they eventually sold for more than £14 million. The Rummer's strange name comes from Romers, which were large drinking glasses popular in the Netherlands and Rhineland up to the seventeenth century.

The **Rhubarb Tavern**, Barton Hill, is believed to be the only pub in the country with that name. It comes from the many rhubarb fields that once covered the area. The Rhubarb, which was originally a house and became a pub in 1880, is the oldest surviving building in the area.

The Hatchet, Frogmore Street, is one of the city's oldest pubs dating back to 1606. It was a haunt of bare-knuckle fighters, who trained there watched by their supporters, and was also well known for cockfighting. The birds were set to take each other on in a pit outside the pub. The Hatchet's front door, with its heavily studded framework, is original and is said to be covered in a layer of human skin preserved by a coat of tar.

Anti-slavery campaigner Thomas Clarkson visited the **Seven Stars** in Thomas Lane in 1787. He collected information from seafarers who were frequenting the pub about conditions on board slave ships. Clarkson passed on the information he collected to William Wilberforce, a politician who led the movement to abolish slavery.

The **King William** alehouse in King Street was built in the seventeenth century as a refuge for poor women. It was later converted into a pub.

The **London Inn**, Canon Street, Bedminster, was originally a rambling eighteenth-century coaching inn that was the first stop for stagecoaches on the journey from Bristol to Wells. In 1864 the *South Bristol Gazette* described the pub as a 'pretentiously named and antiquated hostelry'.

The **Pump House** pub and restaurant at Hotwells was once an essential part of the Floating Harbour. Built in 1871 in the Italianate style, it housed the hydraulic machinery and steam engines that operated the lock gates at the entrance to the harbour. The building has hardly changed and has kept its original name.

SOME FORMER PUBS WITH NEW USES

- The White Hart at Brislington, a coaching inn dating back to 1738, is now the Bristol School of Performing Arts.
- The General Elliott, East Street, Bedminster, has become a fish and chip restaurant.
- The Foresters Arms, Westbury-on-Trym, is now a supermarket.
- The Red Cow, West Street, Bedminster, which could trace its history as an alehouse back to at least 1792, was demolished in 2009 for housing.
- The Magic Box, Stokes Croft, became the home of a comedy club.

EXPANDING BRISTOL

By the early nineteenth century much of Portishead, 9 miles west of Bristol, was owned by the Corporation of Bristol. It had been buying up land there for the previous 300 years, starting with the Manor of North Weston which cost £950. It bought Portishead Dock in 1884.

The Corporation announced construction of Portishead Esplanade in 1893. It was completed by the following summer at a cost of £3,100. The boating lake at the Lake Grounds, once a stagnant stretch of rhynes, was dug out by the unemployed men of Bristol.

Probably the only seaside hotel to have been built by a local authority in the nineteenth century was the Royal Hotel at Portishead. Bristol Corporation had wanted to enhance the area to attract more visitors. The hotel is still trading but under private management.

The training ship *Formidable* was moored off Portishead Pier for more that forty years. It was used to train boys in need of care and protection to lead useful lives. Many of them had been found wandering the streets of Bristol. Some of them did not have a home. When the ship became unseaworthy in 1906, Bristol businessman Henry Fedden built a training school on nearby land. The Grade II listed building has now become a gated development of apartments, houses and maisonettes known as Fedden Village.

STREETS OF HISTORY

Air Balloon Hill, St George
This road is named after an unmanned balloon that landed on the highest spot in St George in 1784 after being launched in Bath.

Alma Road, Clifton
The name comes from the Battle of Alma in the Crimean War of 1854.

Bennett Way, Cumberland Basin
James Bennett was the City Engineer and Planning Officer responsible for development of post-war Bristol.

Christmas Steps, city centre
These forty-nine steps with shops on either side, rising from Host Street to Colston Street, were 'steppered done and finished' in 1669 according to a plaque at the top.

Culver Street, city centre
This street was probably named after a nearby culver or pigeon house.

Cut Throat Lane, St Werburgh's
Two murders were committed here or nearby in 1836 and 1913.

Frogmore Street, city centre
This was once the site of several fishponds.

Molesworth Drive, Bishopsworth
The Revd Walter Molesworth was vicar of Bishopsworth for forty-one years spanning the nineteenth and twentieth centuries.

Nigel Park, Shirehampton
This is named after Nigel Tappenden whose father built houses in the area.

Ninetree Hill, Stokes Croft
This is named after the nine elm trees that once stood there.

Nova Scotia Place, Cumberland Basin
The name marks the signing of the Treaty of Utrecht in 1713 when France ceded Nova Scotia and other territories to England. The Bishop of Bristol had represented Britain at the Congress of Utrecht when the treaty was signed.

Pembroke Road, Clifton
This was once Gallows Acre Lane as it led to the gallows on Clifton Downs. It was changed to its present name in honour of the Earls of Pembroke who were once Lord Lieutenants of Bristol.

Portland Square, St Paul's
This Georgian square was one of the first residential suburbs in Bristol. It takes its name from the Duke of Portland who was Bristol's High Steward in 1787.

Princess Victoria Street, Clifton
This thoroughfare recalls a visit to Clifton by Princess Victoria when she was 11 years old. Previously both ends of the street had different names.

Purdey Road, Fishponds
This name commemorates Victory Purdey, a Methodist preacher from Kingswood known as the 'walking Bible'. He had read the Bible so many times that he could answer any question about it. Purdey, who died in 1822, is said to have preached nearly 3,000 sermons.

Roman Road, Easton
When workmen were laying water pipes in 1870 they unearthed a large quantity of unused Roman coins dated AD 336, thus giving the road its name.

Royal York Crescent, Clifton
This development of forty-six houses was named after Frederick Augustus, Duke of York. The crescent is said to be the longest in Europe at nearly a quarter of a mile long.

Sabrina Way, Stoke Bishop
The road takes its name from the Latin for the River Severn.

Sion Hill, Clifton
This hill, leading up to Clifton Suspension Bridge, is named after the Sion Spring that was discovered at the bottom of the hill. The pump room attached to it later became St Vincent's Rocks Hotel. It is now private residential accommodation.

There and Back Again Lane, Clifton
This is a short cul-de-sac off Berkeley Square. Its name speaks for itself.

Upper Perry Hill, Southville
Perry trees are believed to have grown here. Some historians claim that Elizabeth I had a grandstand view from the top of the hill of a mock battle that was staged for her entertainment on a visit to Bristol in 1574.

Welsh Back, Floating Harbour
For many years this was the centre of trade with ports on the Severn Estuary.

The Zig Zag Path
This steep winding path cut in St Vincent's Rocks near the Clifton Suspension Bridge rises from The Portway at Hotwells to Sion Hill, Clifton. It gets its name from the structure of the path. Princess Victoria is said to have played here when she visited Clifton in 1830 with the Duchess of Kent.

SAINTS, SPIRES AND STEEPLES

BRISTOL CATHEDRAL

Bristol Cathedral evolved from a twelfth-century abbey that was dissolved by Henry VIII in 1538. Three years later he created the Diocese of Bristol with its own cathedral and bishop. The remains of the abbey became a cathedral that is dedicated to the Holy and Undivided Trinity. Henry VIII appointed Paul Bush, who was a King's Chaplain, as the first Bishop of Bristol.

For the first time since its institution during the reign of Edward I, the Royal Maundy Service with all its pomp and pageantry was held at Bristol Cathedral in 1999. As part of the service the queen presented specially minted Maundy Money to twice as many old people as her age in years. All the recipients were being recognised for their service to the Church and the local community.

The ordination of the first women into the Church of England priesthood took place during an historic service at Bristol Cathedral in 1994. This was the culmination of the most bitterly fought battle within the Church since Henry VIII broke away from Rome. The Revd Angela Berners-Wilson has the honour of being the first woman to be ordained when the Bishop of Bristol laid his hands on her head. Altogether thirty-two women were ordained.

Two large candlesticks in the cathedral are named after Robinson Crusoe, the central figure in Daniel Defoe's novel of that name. The candlesticks were given to the cathedral after a privateering voyage by the crews of the *Duke* and *Duchess*, who had been plundering ships around the world of their treasures. They also brought back to Bristol Alexander Selkirk, a sailor who had been marooned on the island of Juan Fernandez in the South Pacific Ocean. His story is said to have inspired Daniel Defoe to write his novel *Robinson Crusoe*.

Crime prevention is nothing new, it seems. The monks who built the staircase to the cathedral's treasury where their silver was kept designed it with a hidden bend to make any burglar fall down and therefore prevent his escape.

Under the seats in the cathedral's choir are misericords on which the monks leaned during the long services. One of them shows a man and a woman fighting over a cooking pot.

The nave, choir and aisles of Bristol Cathedral are all the same height, making it a major example of a 'hall church' in England.

Minor canons at Bristol Cathedral were excused attendance from 7 a.m. prayers from the beginning of November 1761 to the end of March 1762. They had complained that the cold building was 'very dangerous and detrimental to their health'.

A robin that flew into the cathedral in 1772 stayed there until it died fifteen years later. The bird fed itself off the hand of the verger and during services it perched on the organ and joined in the hymn singing.

TRAGEDY OF CATHEDRAL CANON

Tragedy befell the Revd Thomas Newnham, aged 25, a canon of Bristol Cathedral, on 17 March 1775 when he attempted to discover the depth of the Pen Park Hole cavern near Brentry. He was clinging to a branch of a tree to peer down the hole when it suddenly gave way, throwing him about 200ft into a lake at the bottom of the cavern. Although repeated efforts were made to rescue Mr Newnham, his body was not recovered for another six weeks.

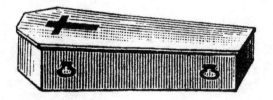

CLIFTON CATHEDRAL

The Roman Catholic Clifton Cathedral was consecrated in 1973 having been built in just three years. This was the fastest such project undertaken in Britain since the Middle Ages. It was also the first cathedral to be built in the West Country since the end of the Second World War.

In his sermon the Archbishop of Westminster, Cardinal Heenan, who consecrated the cathedral, described it as 'the ecclesiastical bargain of the century'. He told the congregation it had cost £600,000. The church replaced the Pro-Cathedral that had stood in Park Place, Clifton, for 125 years. As its title suggested, this was a temporary cathedral.

As a name, Clifton Cathedral is something of a misnomer. Although it stands in the heart of the suburb of Clifton and is the seat of the Bishop of Clifton, it is the 'mother church' of Roman Catholics not only in Bristol but also in the adjoining counties of Somerset, Gloucestershire and Wiltshire. The cathedral is dedicated to the saints Peter and Paul.

Clifton Cathedral was completed in 1973 and was named by the Concrete Society as the best concrete building finished in England that year.

One of the cathedral's architectural features is that the seating in the nave is so arranged that no one in the congregation is more than 50ft from the altar. As there are no pillars in the building everyone has an unobstructed view of the preacher.

RIGHT ROYAL REDCLIFFE

Charles I ordered that the Royal Arms be set up in all parish churches across the land. Most of them have disappeared but the colourful stone Royal Arms at St Mary Redcliffe church still remain over the south door.

Queen Mary made a private visit to St Mary Redcliffe shortly after the outbreak of the Second World War and was shown around the church by the vicar and his churchwardens. Queen Mary was the first queen to visit the church since Elizabeth I in 1574. She had moved out of London to stay with her niece, the Duchess of Beaufort and the Duke of Beaufort at Badminton House, South Gloucestershire, during the war. She became a frequent visitor to Redcliffe church, Bristol Cathedral and many of the city's historic attractions.

On one occasion in 1940, Queen Mary was taking Holy Communion, which delayed the start of a wedding service for a young couple. They were eventually married by the vicar but there was no honeymoon for the couple as the groom was immediately called up for war service.

Queen Mary attended a service with 1,000 members of the Auxiliary Training Service, the women's branch of the British Army, during the Second World War. The service was held in 1943 to mark the fifth anniversary of the organisation.

Princess Margaret, Duchess of Snowdon, unveiled a commemorative plaque at the church during a service in 1965 that marked the completion of restoration work.

Her Royal Highness, the Princess Royal, took a seat in the pews for a service in 1988 marking the 400th anniversary of the return of Church lands by Queen Elizabeth I. They had been seized by Elizabeth's father, Henry VIII, and her brother, Edward VI.

Queen Elizabeth II, accompanied by the Duke of Edinburgh, was given a private tour of the church in 1956 at the start of a day of engagements in and around Bristol. Some 20,000 waited in the churchyard and nearby streets to see the royal couple arrive and leave. In 1995 the queen and the duke were back at St Mary Redcliffe for a service celebrating the work of local charity workers. She told the Revd Tony Whatmough that Redcliffe was 'not the sort of church that you forgot once you had visited it'.

THE WORLD'S FIRST METHODIST CHAPEL

The first Methodist chapel in the world was built by John Wesley on a plot of land at The Horsefair in 1739. It was, and still is, known as the New Room and was the first chapel to be licensed for Methodist preaching. The New Room, with its unusual double-decker pulpit, now nestles between large department stores. It is a Mecca for about 25,000 pilgrims from all over the world who visit the New Room each year.

John Wesley preached in the open air for the first time at the Brickfield, St Philips, in 1739. His last open-air sermon was delivered in King Square in 1790. In between those years Wesley travelled a quarter of a million miles on horseback and preached around 40,000 sermons.

In his journal of 3 October 1755, Wesley says that he left Bristol on horseback for the north Somerset village of Pill which he described as 'a place famous from generation to generation ... for stupid, brutal, abandoned wickedness'.

The Church of England thought John Wesley was too revolutionary and banned him from preaching in many of its pulpits. However, he got around this ruling when he was invited to preach at the Lord Mayor's Chapel, which was under the jurisdiction of Bristol Corporation.

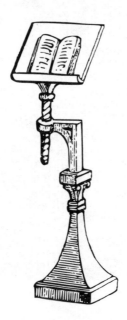

THE OLDEST CHURCH IN THE CITY

Robert, Earl of Gloucester, who was building Bristol Castle with stone from Caen, Normandy, ordered that every tenth stone should be set aside to build the priory church of St James in The Horsefair. The church originally formed part of a Benedictine priory and was completed around 1130. St James Priory has the distinction of being both the city's oldest surviving church and its oldest building.

By AD 1200 there were fifteen churches in and around Bristol. One hundred years later the number had grown to nineteen as well as the Augustinian Abbey (now Bristol Cathedral) and St James Priory. In addition, each of the four Orders of Friars had a house in Bristol.

For many years the only access to St Vincent's chapel was by way of a steep and perilous path down the sheer face of the Avon Gorge. This Roman Catholic chapel was in a natural cavern 90ft below the cliff top. It measured 27ft by 9ft. According to the fifteenth-century Bristol-born topographer William Wyrecester, it took 125 paces to reach the chapel.

Access to the cavern was made easier in 1835 when a 200ft-long tunnel that had been blasted through the limestone rock of the Avon Gorge was opened. Entry to the tunnel was through the observatory, which still stands on Clifton Down. It had taken the owner, William West, two years to excavate the tunnel.

When the spire of Christ Church, Clifton, was completed in 1859, one of the workmen was so delighted that he did a headstand on the quarter-ton capstone 215ft above street level.

George Catcott, an antiquarian, climbed the 205ft steeple of St Nicholas church, overlooking Bristol Bridge, in 1769 to add the finishing touches. Watched by a large crowd of spectators, he placed two pieces of metal, each bearing a Latin inscription, in a cavity prepared for the purpose.

You'll not only need a head for heights but also a pair of sturdy legs to join the choristers of St Stephen's church, city centre, in the ancient tradition of welcoming the first day of May. The choir welcomes May Day with madrigals and other songs on the top of the church's perpendicular tower more than 130ft above street level.

SUBURB'S FIRST CHURCH

The first church to be built in east Bristol for the increasing population in the area was consecrated by the Bishop of Bristol in 1852. Holy Trinity church in St Philips had 2,000 seats, 1,500 of them were free but worshippers had to pay for pews near the front of the church. Holy Trinity, which cost £9,000 to build, closed in 1976 because of dwindling numbers. The building is now a community arts and music centre.

BURNT AT THE STAKE

Heretics against the newly reinstated Catholic faith of Mary Tudor were burnt at the stake at the top of St Michael's Hill. Five Marian Martyrs were burnt there between 1555–1557. The death of the men for the avowal of their Christian faith is recorded on a plaque at Cotham parish church that now stands on the site. They were:

William Shapton	17 October 1555	a weaver
Richard Shapton	17 May 1557	a weaver
Edward Sharpe	8 September 1556	occupation unknown
Thomas Hale	17 May 1557	a shoemaker
Thomas Bennion	17 August 1557	a carpenter

CHURCH CURIOSITIES

Smallest place of worship

Standing at the top of Christmas Steps is the only church in the country dedicated to the Three Kings of Cologne – Caspar, Balthasar and Melchior – also known as the Biblical Magi and the Three Wise Men. The church was built in the fifteenth century along with the adjoining almshouse (now private accommodation) by John Foster, a mayor and a merchant of Bristol. The church is said to be based on the shrine of The Magi in Cologne Cathedral. It is one of Bristol's smallest places of worship, measuring just 18 by 22ft.

Church with no name

Redland chapel is one of the few churches not to be dedicated to a patron saint. It was built in 1743 as a private chapel costing £850 for the local manor house, Redland Court, which is now Redland High School. In 1942 the Anglican parish of Redland was formed and the chapel became the parish church but it has never been dedicated to a saint.

Church on the move

The fifteenth-century church of St Werburgh's, which stood on the corner of Small Street and Corn Street, was taken down stone by stone in the nineteenth century to make way for road widening. Each stone was numbered and carted several miles across the city to Mina Road. The entire operation of demolition and reconstruction took two years, with the first services being held at Mina Road in autumn 1879. The church, which is now used as a rock-climbing centre, gave its name to the district.

Church built on an arch

The church of St John the Baptist, now redundant as a place of worship, is unusual because it sits astride St John's Arch, Broad Street. Neither does the church have any east or west windows. The arch, which once had a portcullis, is the only remaining ancient gateway that gave entry to Bristol. At one time the vicar of St John's used an hourglass by which he timed his sermons.

A watery boundary

The parish boundaries of St Stephen's church, city centre, stretch out to the Severn Estuary to take in the islands of Steep Holm and Flat Holm.

Unusual roof supports

A distinctive feature of St Mary Redcliffe church is the 1,000 gilded bosses in the roof vaulting – all of which are believed to be different. The bosses include a maze, green men, a monster biting its own tail and a mermaid with traditional long tresses holding a comb in one hand and a mirror in the other.

Explorer's gift

St Mary Redcliffe also has, as one of its treasures, a 4ft-long whale bone that the explorer John Cabot brought back from his voyage of discovery to North America. It is on display high up on a wall near a model of Cabot's ship the *Matthew*. In medieval days explorers often returned to a church with a gift in thanksgiving for a safe journey.

Bishop's coach stoned

Protestors were out in force when the Bishop of Bath and Wells consecrated St Paul's church, Southville, in 1831. Stones and mud were thrown at his carriage as he left the church on Coronation Road. Protestors didn't like the bishop's opposition to the Reform Bill that was going through Parliament at the time.

Church with a double

A replica of Christ Church, Clifton, has been built in Thames Town, a suburb of Shanghai in China. It is built in a style that is imitative of English architecture.

An unusual saint

A saint with a rather strange background was remembered by congregations at St Mary-Le-Port church that had a chapel and altar dedicated to St Wilgefortis. She was also known as Saint Uncumber and was the patron saint of unhappily married women. Apparently, she had taken a vow of chastity and is said to have grown a beard to cover her beauty and put off men who might contemplate marrying her. The cult of St Wilgefortis was extremely popular in late medieval Europe but she may well be one of those saints who never existed.

LEST WE FORGET

There are more parishioners lying at rest in the city's churchyards than there are sitting in the church pews. As churchyards around the city became overcrowded – in some graves there were three or even four bodies – the Bristol General Cemetery Company was formed with a capital of £15,000 in £20 shares.

The proprietors of Arnos Vale cemetery opened it on a steep 45-acre hillside between the Bath and Wells Roads in south-east Bristol. The site was originally earmarked as the home of Bristol Zoo but its founders opted for a site on the edge of Clifton Downs instead.

In the first ten years or so the number of burials at Arnos Vale was low but numbers increased with the passing of the 1848 Public Health Act. This barred further burials at twenty-six churchyards and private burial grounds around the city. Included in this ruling was Bristol Infirmary's burial ground for paupers who died in hospital. More than 150,000 people are now buried at Arnos Vale. It is now the city's largest cemetery.

Mary Breillat, who died on 23 July 1839 aged 68, was the first person to be buried at Arnos Vale. She was interred in a Nonconformist section of the cemetery. Her grave is distinctive because of its 12ft-high obelisk. Mrs Breillat was the wife of John Breillat who set up the Bristol Gas Lighting Company in 1816. Four years later most of the city's main streets were lit by coal gas.

Twenty-seven monuments and memorials at Arnos Vale cemetery are listed as Grade II* on the UK register of buildings and structures of architectural importance. They include monuments commemorating the lives of some notable people including Rajah Rammohun Roy, who was regarded as the founder of modern India. He died from meningitis while visiting Bristol in 1833. Initially, Rajah Roy was buried in the grounds of his host's home at Stapleton but ten years later was reinterred at Arnos Vale cemetery. His tomb is designed along the lines of a Hindu temple.

One hundred carriages followed the hearse of George Muller for his funeral at Arnos Vale in 1898. Thousands of people also lined the funeral route. Muller, a Prussian, had died aged 92. He spent most of his life in Bristol where he had founded a number of large orphanages at Ashley Down for children abandoned on the streets or in workhouses.

About 2,000 people, many of them tobacco workers, paid their last respects to William Day Wills at his funeral at Arnos Vale. He died after being struck by a horse-drawn bus while he was crossing the road in Snow Hill, London, in 1865.

TOMBSTONES WITH A DIFFERENCE

The tomb of William Humpage at Arnos Vale is most unusual as it takes the form of a steam boiler. A cross on the top is in the shape of a torque wrench. Humpage died from Spanish Flu when he was 29 years old. He is buried with other members of his family with an unusual inscription on the tombstone: 'We whacked the Huns.'

A tombstone in the south churchyard of St Mary Redcliffe bearing the dates 1912–1927 marks the grave of the church cat. Apparently, he so liked the welcome he received after strolling through the Priest's Door that he decided to spend the rest of his life in the church. The cat often sat beside the organist while he played during services. When the cat died, the church organised a funeral with the vicar officiating and the choir singing at the graveside.

According to a tombstone in St Luke's churchyard, Brislington, Thomas Newman was 153 years old when he died in 1542. Did the stonemason add the figure '1' to 53 by mistake without anyone spotting it or did Mr Newman really live to such a grand old age? The inscription adds: 'This stone was new faced in the year 1771 to perpetuate the great age of the deceased.'

5

WARTIME MATTERS

THE BRISTOL WARSHIP

Seven ships of the Royal Navy have been named after Bristol. The first was built in 1653 on the orders of Oliver Cromwell for his Commonwealth navy. She was equipped with forty-eight guns and had a complement of 230 men. Rather oddly, the name Bristol on the side of the ship was spelt with two 'l's. After an extraordinarily long career the ship foundered in the English Channel in 1709 with the loss of twenty lives.

The second ship to take the name of Bristol to sea was launched in 1711. She carried fifty guns and had a complement of 350 sailors. The ship saw service in various theatres of war for more than half a century before being taken to the breaker's yard in 1768.

A successor ship was launched in 1773 and three years later was serving in the American War of Independence. The ship eventually returned to Great Britain to be converted into a hospital ship before being broken up in 1810.

The fourth HMS *Bristol* was not always known by that name. While this East Indiaman was being built in 1796 the ship was known as the *Earl Talbot*. The Admiralty bought the vessel while it was still under construction and by the time of its launch it had become HMS *Agincourt*. The ship was later renamed HMS *Bristol* but had a short life under that name, being sold five years later in 1814.

It was almost half a century before another HMS *Bristol* was launched in 1861. For most of her life the ship was used as a seagoing training vessel for cadets. This was a wooden screw-frigate with a complement of 600 men. The ship went to the breaker's yard in 1883.

The sixth HMS *Bristol* was launched in 1910 and, after seeing service in the First World War, it was sold in 1921.

The last ship to bear the name was a guided missile-armed destroyer that was commissioned at Avonmouth Docks in 1973. The ship was in service for eighteen years and with her 600 men played an important part in the Falkland Islands war in 1982 when she became a flagship of the task force. It was the only Type 82 destroyer built by the Royal Navy and cost more than £25 million. HMS *Bristol* has been decommissioned and converted into a training ship moored at Portsmouth Harbour.

'BRISTOL'S OWN' REGIMENT

Soon after the First World War was declared the Bristol Citizens Recruiting Committee was set up. The city, showing a streak of independence, raised its own regiment that quickly became known as 'Bristol's Own'. Lord Kitchener, Secretary of State for War, sanctioned 'the enrolment of names of single men of the city of Bristol and neighbourhood between the ages of 19–35 who are willing to join the Colours for the duration of the war'. Eventually, 'Bristol's Own' became the 12th Battalion Gloucestershire Regiment.

Frederick Weatherley, a leading barrister, author and lyricist who lived in Portishead, was so moved by the number of men who volunteered for war service that he wrote a patriotic recruiting song he called *Bravo Bristol!* It was one of 3,000 songs, half of which were published, that Weatherley wrote. The well-known composer Ivor Novello wrote the music for *Bravo Bristol!*

More than 1,300 men joined 'Bristol's Own'. They did some of their training at the site of an international exhibition that had been set up on Ashton Meadows and became known as the White City. Its white pavilions, which housed various exhibitions celebrating the city's history and its industry and commerce, were converted into temporary barracks for the soldiers.

'Bristol's Own' took part in most of the major battles in France, Flanders and Italy between 1915 and 1918 when the regiment was disbanded in September of that year, two months before the war ended. The regiment gained twenty-two battle honours but unfortunately more than 700 men never returned home. Many others were injured.

WAR WORK

The British and Colonial Aeroplane Company that was founded by entrepreneur Sir George White in 1910, played a major part in the First World War. By the outbreak of hostilities White's company had produced many trainer aircraft for its two flying schools that provided many of the pilots available for war service. His firm built almost 1,300 Be2 planes, 374 Bristol Scouts and more than 5,000 Bristol Fighters which saw war service.

In the First World War the family-owned motorcycle firm of Douglas of Kingswood won a major order to make around 70,000 motorcycles for military use. Many of the machines were used by despatch riders on the rough and rugged terrain of the Western Front. After the war several members of the Royal Family bought Douglas motorbikes. The firm was bought out in 1957 by the Westinghouse Brake and Signal Company of Chippenham, bringing to an end fifty years of motorcycle production.

More than 1,000 people, mostly women and girls, were employed by the Ministry of Munitions at a factory it had specially built at Chittening near Avonmouth. The women were employed to fill shells with the deadly mustard gas which the Germans introduced into the war and had killed thousands of soldiers. Ironically, the mustard gas from Chittening arrived in France less than two months before the Armistice.

The factory had its own hospital and nursing staff that reported that there were 1,400 illnesses amongst 1,100 workers, some having more than one disease. Three people died in accidents at the factory and four more as a result of their illnesses.

During the war the company that ran the tram services in Bristol employed for the first time women as conductresses or, as they were called, clippies. Their job was to collect fares from passengers and in return give them a ticket that would be clipped, preventing it from being used again. All went well until the end of the war when returning soldiers wanted their jobs back as conductors. The clippies refused and in April 1920 about 2,000 people gathered outside the tram company's office to support the men. Some ugly scenes developed, with trams being damaged. All the clippies lost their jobs but the tramways bosses paid them off with £5 each.

'WE WILL REMEMBER THEM'

Eight members of the armed services who were awarded the Victoria Cross – the highest military decoration awarded for valour 'in the face of the enemy' – are remembered at cemeteries across Bristol:

Lt-Col Frederick Bell of the West Australian Mounted Infantry won the VC in the Boer War in 1901. He died in 1954 and is buried at Canford cemetery, Westbury-on-Trym.

Lt-Col Ferdinand Le Quesne, a surgeon with the Royal Army Medical Corps, was awarded the VC in Burma in 1889. He died in 1950 and his grave can be found at Canford cemetery.

Acting L/Cpl Frederick Room of the Royal Irish Regiment was honoured with the VC in Belgium in 1917 when he was only 22 years old. He died in 1932 and is buried at Greenbank cemetery.

Bgdr Manley James of the Gloucestershire Regiment was awarded the VC in France in 1918. He died in 1975 and is buried at Canford cemetery.

Lt-Col Daniel Burges, who was with the Gloucestershire Regiment, was recognised for his services in the Balkans. He died in 1946 and has a memorial plaque at Arnos Vale cemetery.

Col John Daunt of the Bengal Military Police received the VC in the Indian Mutiny. He died in 1886 and is buried at Redland Parish Church Graveyard.

Maj.-Gen. Gronow Davis of the Royal Regiment of Artillery received his VC in Crimea. He was invested with it at the first investiture of the medal by Queen Victoria in Hyde Park in June 1857. Gronow Davis died in 1891 and is buried at Arnos Vale cemetery.

L/Sgt Harry Wood of the Scots Guards was awarded his VC in France in 1918. He died in 1924 and is buried at Arnos Vale cemetery.

WAR MEMORIAL DISAGREEMENTS

The people of Bristol had to wait fourteen years after the First World War ended in 1918 for a civic memorial to the city's fallen. Bristol had sent out around 55,000 men to the Western Front but about 6,000 of them never returned.

A war memorial committee was headed by the Lord Mayor but talks quickly broke down. A new committee was formed but again there was disagreement about what form a memorial should take, how it would be funded and where it would stand. Eventually it was agreed that Colston Avenue, also known at the time as Magpie Park, would be the site.

A competition for a suitable memorial was launched amongst local architects. Eighteen entries were submitted and a cenotaph similar to the one in Whitehall was selected. The cenotaph was eventually unveiled in 1932 by Field Marshall Sir William Birdwood, watched by some 50,000 people. Bristol was one of the last of the major cities in Great Britain to have a civic memorial.

HEALING THE INJURED

Various eminent families gave over their homes to become makeshift war hospitals. Robert Bush, who owned Bishop's Knoll house at Sneyd Park, converted his home into a hospital in just three weeks at his own expense. There was room for 100 wounded soldiers. Mr Bush, who had worked in Australia as a sheep farmer, insisted the hospital's patients should be Australian. He even went to meet the wounded soldiers on their arrival in Bristol.

Ashton Court mansion in the south of the city became a temporary hospital, as did a lunatic asylum at Fishponds and the workhouse at Southmead.

The girls at Red Maids' School at Westbury-on-Trym moved out of their dormitories to make way for wounded servicemen. The girls were given accommodation at Bristol University's Manor Hall in Clifton.

Nearly 70,000 injured soldiers arrived at Temple Meads station by ambulance trains during the First World War. Another 25,000 were brought into the city by ships that berthed at Avonmouth Docks.

BOMBS OVER BRISTOL

Bristol was the fifth most heavily bombed city in England in the Second World War with a total of seventy-seven air raids. The first air-raid siren warning was sounded shortly after midnight on 25 June 1940. It was heard for the last time on 13 June 1944.

During the war 1,299 people lost their lives in what became known as the Bristol Blitz. A further 1,303 suffered serious injuries while 2,002 were slightly injured. A plaque to the memory of civilians who lost their lives is on the wall of the bombed ruins of St Peter's church, Castle Park. The church itself, all but for its walls and tower, was reduced to rubble.

So many people died in the various air raids that there were communal burials at Greenbank cemetery, which commemorates 129 Second World War casualties. A German Luftwaffe crew killed during the Bristol Blitz also have a grave at Greenbank.

A total of 89,080 buildings were hit by enemy action during the war. This included 81,830 houses that were destroyed or extensively damaged.

An estimated 5,000 incendiaries were dropped during the first major air raid on 24 November 1940, which destroyed the centre of the city. The Castle Street shopping centre (now Castle Park) was wiped out; many churches and public buildings, including the museum, art gallery and Bristol University, were either destroyed or badly damaged. Bristol Fire Brigade was reinforced by crews from seventy-seven brigades from neighbouring counties, with an additional 20,000ft of hose from Cardiff, Newport Bournemouth and Plymouth.

One of the worst bombing attacks happened on 28 August 1942 when a 500lb bomb dropped on Broad Weir. Three buses collecting passengers immediately caught alight and forty-five people were killed. Another fifty-six people were injured.

A direct hit by an enemy bomb on St Paul's church, Southville, on Good Friday 1941 left only its four walls and tower standing. Remarkably, 300 people who had sought refuge in the crypt were unhurt. Many of them described it at the time as a 'modern miracle'. Ten weddings due to take place at St Paul's on the Saturday were transferred to another church.

A large amount of rubble from Bristol's bombed buildings was exported to America. Ships took out the rubble as ballast for New York where it was used in the foundations of Bristol Basin, New York. More rubble was used in the reclamation of land at Avonmouth Docks. Some 30 acres of it formed the foundations of a new sea terminal for petroleum tankers.

TAKEN TO A PLACE OF SAFETY

A total of 20,085 children were evacuated from the city, mainly to Devon and Cornwall, during the Blitz. They were all back home by the end of 1944.

Senior pupils at Clifton College were taken to hotels in Bude, north Cornwall, and those in the prep school were moved to historic Butcombe Court in north Somerset, as soldiers from the American army moved into their classrooms from 1942 onwards to make arrangements for the D-Day landings on 6 June 1944.

A dozen colleges of Oxford University offered rest holidays during the academic vacation to Bristolians who had suffered sleepless nights because of the constant bombing. During the Blitz students from King's College, London, moved out of the capital into Bristol.

WARTIME RACE ROW

During the war black and white American soldiers were segregated in their leisure time. Tensions between the soldiers built up and on 15 July 1944 fighting broke out between more than 400 black and white American troops in Park Street. The black troops were incensed at being barred from what they thought were the best nightclubs in town. The military police were called in to break up the fighting and one of them was stabbed in the leg. Several black GIs were injured and one of them later died.

BRISTOL WAR EFFORT

Burwalls House, a Grade II listed mansion at the Somerset end of Clifton Suspension Bridge, played an important part in the defence of Bristol in the Second World War. The house had been requisitioned by the War Office and became the headquarters of the Heavy Anti-Aircraft Regiment. Its batteries defended Bristol and its port from enemy action. Burwalls was built by Joseph Leech, owner of the *Bristol Times* newspaper. After he died it was bought by members of the Wills tobacco family. Plans are underway to redevelop the house and outbuildings into residential accommodation.

Campbell's White Funnel Bristol Channel steamers based in Bristol all served in the Second World War. Some of them were given new names to avoid confusion with existing navy ships. Eight steamers were at Dunkirk, three were destroyed, two others were sunk and two were scrapped. Only three were able to return to the day-trip trade taking families to coastal resorts in Devon, Somerset and South Wales.

The Wills tobacco family provided prime oak from their country estate at Batsford Park, Gloucestershire, for repairs to war-damage at the Great Hall of Bristol University's Wills Memorial Building. The timber was used to restore its hammer-beam roof, which was gutted in 1940. Restoration was completed twenty-three years later when the Great Hall was reopened in the presence of Sir Winston Churchill, the university's chancellor.

A number of so-called community restaurants, officially known as British Restaurants, opened across the city during the Second World War. They were set up by the Ministry of Food and run on a non-profit-making basis by local committees. The restaurants ensured that those who had run out of food-rationing coupons were still able to get a meal. A typical three-course meal at the restaurant on College Green cost 1*s* 9*d*.

MEMORIALS OF WAR

The ruins of three bombed churches in the centre of the city remain both as monuments to the city's civilian dead and a reminder of the horrors of war. St Peter's, St Mary Le Port, both on what is now Castle Park, and Temple church, off Victoria Street, were all bombed during the first major German raid of 24/25 November 1940.

A star-shaped light in the ceiling of St George's Music Centre marks the point where an incendiary bomb that failed to ignite crashed through the roof. St George's, on the edge of Brandon Hill Park, was an Anglican church until the 1970s when it was made redundant because of a dwindling congregation.

6

PEOPLE WHO PUT
BRISTOL ON THE MAP

Electors in the Bristol Central constituency voted into office the city's first female Member of Parliament in a by-election in 1942. She was Lady Violet Apsley, the Conservative Party candidate, who succeeded her late husband in the seat. Lady Apsley represented the constituency at Westminster until 1945 when it was taken by the Labour candidate at the General Election.

Banksy is Bristol's – and Britain's – most prolific and best-known graffiti artist. Although we know he was born in the city we don't know his real name, where he was educated, or where he lives, for Banksy fiercely guards his identity. He started creating graffiti when he was a teenager and quickly became part of the local, then national and now the international graffiti scene.

Edward Hodges Bailey (1788–1867), who was born at Downend, developed a taste for art at an early age. He amused his peers at Bristol Grammar School by modelling wax portraits of them. This may not have helped him with his academic studies but at the age of 16 he was working in a sculptor's studio in London. Bailey went on to become a prolific sculptor in his own right. Amongst his many works is the 17ft-high statue of Admiral Nelson standing on the top of Nelson's column in Trafalgar Square.

Tony Benn was the Member of Parliament for Bristol South East for thirty years from 1950 although there was a gap of nearly two years. On inheriting his father's title of Viscount Stansgate in 1961 Tony Benn was prevented from continuing as a Member of Parliament. He successfully ran a campaign to renounce the title and on the day that the 1963 Peerage Act came into force he disclaimed the peerage. He won back his old seat at a by-election, eventually losing it to a Conservative candidate in the General Election of 1983.

Elizabeth Blackwell, who was born at Counterslip in 1821, became the first woman in the world to qualify as a doctor, albeit in America in 1849. When she was 11 years old, Elizabeth's family moved from Bristol to America where she later studied at Geneva Medical College, New York State. She came top of her class, graduating with a medical degree. Elizabeth eventually returned to England and set up a medical college for women.

Richard Bright (1789–1858), who was born in Queen Square, studied medicine and is best known for his findings on the kidney disease named after him – Bright's Disease – which were published in 1827. At the start of Queen Victoria's reign he was appointed Royal Physician Extraordinary.

Alderman Mrs Florence Brown made local government history in 1963 when she became the city's first female Lord Mayor. Mrs Brown's husband was her official escort for her year of office. Mrs Brown had previously served on various council committees for a number of years.

Unknowingly Louise Brown made international history when she arrived in the world in July 1978. Louise had the distinction of being the world's first so-called test-tube baby. Her parents, Lesley and John, then living in Easton, had taken part in the pioneering work of two doctors involving assisted conception through invitro fertilisation. Louise, who tipped the scales at 5lb 12oz, has herself married and given birth – naturally – to her own daughter.

The explorer Giovanni Caboto, better known as John Cabot, his son Sebastian and a crew of eighteen local men sailed from the harbour in Bristol in 1497 in his caravel *The Matthew*. He was hoping to discover trading routes with Asia, however, he crossed the Atlantic and made landfall fifty-three days later at Newfoundland, North America. He returned to Bristol to the welcome of church bells ringing from the many towers around the harbour.

sebastian cabot

Aeronautical engineer Don Cameron gave up a career in the aircraft industry to set up a business in the basement of his home making hot-air balloons. He now has a factory in Bedminster where he employs nearly sixty people designing and making balloons for competitive flying, for pleasure and for firms wanting special shapes for corporate publicity. Cameron's business has led to Bristol being dubbed the 'balloon capital of the world'.

William Canynge the Younger was the biggest shipowner and employer in Bristol in the fifteenth century with nine ships and nearly 900 men on his books. He used his wealth to help rebuild St Mary Redcliffe church. After his wife died, Canynge gave up all his worldly possessions and trained for Holy Orders. He was eventually appointed Dean of Westbury-on-Trym College. Canynge, who died aged 72, has two monuments in St Mary Redcliffe church. Both have an effigy of him; one depicts him lying by his wife's side while the other shows him on his own wearing priest's robes.

Bristol University was the first British university to appoint a woman as head of its governing body when Mrs Stella Clarke was elected chairman of its council in 1985. She held the post for twelve years. Mrs Clarke, who had been active in public life for sixty years, working with national and local bodies, was later awarded an Honorary Fellowship by the university, the highest honour it can grant.

Edward Colston (1636–1721) is widely regarded as one of the city's greatest benefactors, although he spent most of his life in London. He gave away about £75,000; an immense amount at the time. A dozen streets are named after Colston, as are schools, charities and the almshouses he founded and which still survive. He made his fortune trading in wine and cloth but was also involved in the slave trade. Although now viewed with great abhorrence, the slave trade was legal at the time. When Colston died, aged 84, church bells in Bristol tolled non-stop for around sixteen hours. He was buried in All Saints church, off Corn Street.

Consultant paediatrician Dr Beryl Corner was a pioneer in the field of obstetrics in the face of strong prejudice from male colleagues. She set up the first premature baby unit at Southmead Hospital in 1946. Dr Corner cared for the world's first quadruplets – Bridget, Frances, Elizabeth and Jennifer Good – who were born by caesarean section at Southmead in 1948. Almost up until her death in 2007 at the age of 96 Dr Corner was still taking an interest in medical matters and attending conferences.

Paul Dirac (1902–1984) attended Cotham School and went on to study engineering and physics at Cambridge University, where he became Professor of Mathematics. His main field was quantum mechanics. Dirac was a joint winner of the 1933 Nobel Prize in physics awarded for 'the discovery of new productive forms of atomic theory'.

By the age of 28, Keith Floyd owned and ran three restaurants in the Clifton and Redland districts. He was spotted by a BBC producer and went on to make twenty-six series of television programmes ranging from six to twelve episodes. He also wrote books that combined cooking and travel information. Floyd died suddenly in 2009, aged 65, at the home of his partner in Dorset shortly after a meal that included oysters and partridge with champagne.

Flt Lt Michelle Goatman, who was born in Bristol in 1976 and was educated at Bristol Grammar School, was the first woman – and so far the only one – to be awarded the Distinguished Flying Cross. She received the honour in 2007 while serving in Iraq with the Royal Air Force.

Dr William Gilbert Grace (1848–1915), born in Downend, is best remembered for his cricketing skills rather than his use of the stethoscope. Grace, who qualified as a doctor in 1879, was born into a cricketing family and played his first game for West Gloucestershire against Bedminster when he was just 9 years old. During his first-class cricketing career Grace made 126 centuries, scored 54,896 runs and took 2,864 wickets. He was known as the 'Master of Cricket'.

Thomas Lawrence, who was born in Red Cross Street, Old Market, in 1769, had a precocious talent as a child for sketching and painting customers in the pub his father ran. By the age of 12 he even had his own studio. Lawrence was eventually appointed 'Painter in Ordinary' to King George II and was knighted in 1815. Five years later he was appointed President of the Royal Academy.

Vincent Lean was a barrister who, when he died aged 79 in 1899, left £50,000 in his will for the Central Library at College Green to built. He also bequeathed his collection of 5,000 books to the library, which opened in 1906 without any cost to the city's ratepayers.

Sir Bernard Lovell (1913–2012), who came from Oldland Common, studied at Bristol University and eventually became professor of radio astronomy at Manchester. He was later appointed director of Jodrell Bank experimental station. The school that Lovell attended near his home is now named after him.

The oldest person to have ever been granted an honorary degree by Bristol University to date has been Harry Patch. He was made an Honorary Master of Arts in 2005 when he was 107 years old. Mr Patch had worked on the university's Wills Memorial Building and was a veteran of the First World War. Indeed, he was the last surviving soldier known to have fought in the trenches on the Western Front. He died in 2009, five weeks after his 111th birthday. An Avon and Somerset police horse has also been named after Harry.

Welcoming the sixty-nine boys on the register for the first term at Clifton College in September 1862, headmaster Dr John Percival told them he wanted to build a school that would turn out boys who would be 'brave, gentlemanly, Christian and classically educated'. Percival spent sixteen years at Clifton helping to make it one of Britain's best-known public schools. He was later appointed Bishop of Hereford. His love for the college was so great that he requested to be buried in the vault of the college chapel, although this was illegal; it was not licensed for burials.

Mary Perkins, who was born on St Michael's Hill, developed an interest in eye care when, as a teenage schoolgirl, she helped her father on Saturday's in his optician's business in the centre of the city. After training to be an optometrist, Mary and her husband founded the Specsavers Optical Group in 1984. It is now a global business. Mary Perkins was made a Dame in 2007, the first female optician in the UK to be granted this honour.

Former businesswoman Mary Prior is the first woman to hold the post of Lord Lieutenant of the County of Bristol. The office itself was created by Henry III and each holder of it is the queen's representative for his or her particular county. Amongst her many civic duties, Mrs Prior, who was appointed in 2007, welcomes members of the Royal Family when they visit Bristol. Her role is non-political and unpaid.

Bodybuilder David Prowse, who was brought up in Southmead, played Darth Vader in the original *Star Wars* films, although the voice of his character was spoken by another actor. Prowse is also known as the Green Cross Code Man, a superhero character invented in the 1970s to promote road safety amongst children by getting them to look twice before crossing the road.

It is said that Michael Redgrave was given his first name because his mother could see the tower of the church of St Michael's-on-the-Mount-Without from her maternity bed. The boy's interest in drama led him to become one of Britain's greatest classical actors. He was educated at Clifton College where the school's theatre is named after him. Redgrave was knighted for his services to theatre. He died in 1985 aged 77.

Mary Robinson (1758–1800), who was born in a house near Bristol Cathedral, became an actress, poet, dramatist and novelist. During her lifetime she was known as Perdita after the character she played in Shakespeare's *The Winter's Tale*. More notoriety came her way when she became mistress of King George IV while he was still Prince of Wales.

The notorious pirate known as Blackbeard (aka Edward Teach) is said to have been born near Redcliffe Wharf. He went on to lead a reign of terror across the Caribbean Sea and the Atlantic Ocean where he captured hundreds of ships. He would ransack them for any valuables and set them alight. Blackbeard came to a grisly end during a skirmish at sea when he was shot five times, stabbed more than twenty times and decapitated. It's said that his head was hung on the ship's rigging while his corpse was tossed overboard.

The first consulate to be set up in Bristol was the American consulate which was opened in 1792, just three years after George Washington had been created the first president of the United States of America. The consul in Bristol was Elias Vanderhorst, from South Carolina. However, he and his family had been living in the city for the previous eighteen years.

Sir George White (1854–1916) not only left his mark on his native Bristol by setting up the British and Colonial Aeroplane Company at Filton but was also a pioneer of electric tramways across England and was president of the Bristol Stock Exchange. He left school at the age of 15 and started work in a solicitor's office.

John Whitson arrived in Bristol in his early years virtually penniless. However, he went on to become a wealthy merchant and Member of Parliament for Bristol and was twice its mayor. In his will Whitson left his wealth to set up a girls' school. He stipulated that the students should be 'apparelled in red', hence the school's name of Red Maids. The school at Westbury-on-Trym was founded in 1634, which makes it the oldest girls' school in the country. Once a year, the school's 600 girls, some wearing their traditional red cloaks and white bonnets, process through the city to attend a Founder's Day service at Bristol Cathedral.

Canon Wendy Wilby was the first female member of the clergy to ever hold office at Bristol Cathedral. She was appointed its Canon Precentor in 2007 and also became Dean of Women's Ministry. Canon Wilby retired in 2013.

Henry Overton Wills of the tobacco family promised in 1908 that he would give £100,000 towards the endowment of Bristol University provided a charter was granted within two years. The following year King Edward VII granted the charter, which made University College, founded in 1876, a university entitled to award degrees. As a memorial to Henry Wills, his sons, Henry and George, built a 215ft neo-Gothic tower they called the Wills Memorial Building. It is part of the university's campus.

Bristol-born William Wyrcestre (or Worcestre) was a topographer who travelled around England measuring the size of towns and their buildings. His measurements of buildings, especially fifteenth-century churches in Bristol, were so accurate that restorers were able to make ruined buildings look just like the original.

7

THE CITY
AT WORK

One of the city's oldest industries is that of glassmaking. Bristol was once famed for its blue glass. By the eighteenth century it was the leading glassmaking centre in England with kilns galore belching out thick black smoke in the adjoining suburbs of Redcliffe and Temple. More than half the bottles and window glass in the country was made in Bristol. Such was the fame of the glassblowers that they were invited to show off their skills at the Great Exhibition of the Works of Industry of All Nations at Crystal Palace in 1851.

The glass industry gradually declined in the second half of the nineteenth century thanks to an economic recession. The last kiln to close was in 1922. The only remnant of the industry is the base of a kiln at Redcliffe that has been converted into a hotel restaurant. However, the industry was revived in the 1980s and glass is still being blown in the traditional way.

WORLD'S FIRST LEAD SHOT TOWER

William Watts was a plumber who devised a method of making completely spherical lead shot, much in demand for military use at the time. His plan was to drop molten lead from a height of some 100ft into a pan of water. To achieve this he turned his home on Redcliffe Hill into the world's first lead shot tower. That was in 1872 and it stood there until 1979 when it was demolished to make way for road widening. Another tower was built at St Philips where lead shot continued to be made until 1995.

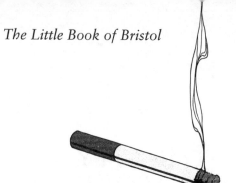

TOBACCO BARONS

Henry Overton Wills, the son of a Salisbury watchmaker, arrived in Bristol in 1786 and founded the family-run tobacco firm of W.D. and H.O. Wills in a converted house in Redcliffe Street.

In the firm's early days, women applying for work with Wills had to provide a Sunday school reference and pass a sewing test to prove their dexterity for production-line work.

In its heyday in the 1970s, Wills employed more than 4,500 people in Bristol alone, who produced more than 350 million cigarettes a week. Its purpose-built factory on a 56-acre landscaped site at Hartcliffe was the largest tobacco factory in Europe.

Wills' most popular cigarette was the Woodbine, which was especially favoured by British soldiers serving in the trenches in the First World War.

At the start of the twentieth century, Wills, along with other British tobacco manufacturers, faced competition from American rivals. This led to Wills merging with thirteen British firms to form the Imperial Tobacco Company to fight off any takeover bid. Sir William Wills was Imperial's founding chairman.

In 1970 the daily payment that Wills made to HM Customs and Excise in tobacco duty amounted to approximately £850,000.

As the anti-smoking health campaign got under way in 1977, Imperial Tobacco Company launched three new brands of cigarettes containing about 25 per cent of what it called New Smoking Material (NSM). The cigarettes, which were developed in Bristol, contained less tobacco and a substitute material that smokers could puff on. Despite a massive national publicity campaign, NSM cigarettes never took off and more than 100 million of them had to be destroyed.

The sole reminder of Bristol's tobacco trade is a theatre space called the Tobacco Factory where everything from new productions to Shakespeare are staged. The building was once a tobacco factory.

SWEET STORY OF SUCCESS

Joseph Fry, an apothecary with a shop in Small Street, was making his own chocolate, initially as a drink, in 1756. The firm of Fry's eventually made the first block of chocolate in the world.

The demand for chocolate was so great that J.S. Fry & Sons built seven factories in Bristol. By the start of the twentieth century they employed 4,600 people, mostly women, who were known as 'Fry's Angels'. All staff were expected to attend a service at the start of the day and hymn singing was encouraged during the working shift of around twelve hours.

One of Fry's best-known brands was the 'Five Boys' chocolate bar, probably because of its unusual wrapper. This had five pictures of a boy's face in various states of emotion. The pictures were titled Desperation, Pacification, Expectation, Acclamation and Realisation.

Fry's merged with rival chocolate maker Cadbury in 1919 but still kept its name. It moved out of its Bristol factories to the Cadbury plant at Somerdale, Keynsham, 7 miles away.

In 2009 Cadbury's announced the closure of the factory, transferring production to Poland.

BRISTOL ABOVE THE CLOUDS

Filton, once a village a mile or two north of Bristol, could arguably be called the birthplace of the British aircraft manufacturing industry. It all started in 1910 when industrialist and entrepreneur Sir George White set up the British and Colonial Aircraft Company there with his own money in a disused tramcar depot.

The first successful aircraft built by Sir George's firm was the Bristol Boxkite biplane of which eighty were built. It was given a public demonstration over Clifton Downs and Clifton Suspension Bridge by French pilot Maurice Tetard in 1910. A replica of the Boxkite hangs from the ceiling of Bristol Museum's entrance hall. It was built for the 1965 film *Those Magnificent Men and their Flying Machines*. Since the days of the Boxkite more than 15,000 aircraft have been built at Filton.

The firm later became Bristol Aeroplane Company and in 1959 it merged with several other aircraft manufacturers to form the British Aircraft Corporation. At one time more than 40,000 people worked in the aircraft industry at Filton.

The largest plane to have been built in Britain at the time made its maiden flight from Filton in 1949. The wingspan of the Brabazon was 230ft and its length was 1,777ft. It was designed to carry 100 passengers across the Atlantic in luxury. The plane was so big that Filton's neighbouring village of Charlton, home to some thirty families, was demolished to make way for a lengthened runway. However, no one wanted the Brabazon so the government scrapped the plane four years after its first flight.

One of the aircraft built at Filton after the war was the Bristol Britannia, also known as the 'Whispering Giant' because of its size and quiet engine. The Britannia made the first non-stop flight from London to Canada's Pacific Coast in 1957 in fourteen hours forty minutes.

The Brabazon hangar became the assembly hall for the world's first supersonic aircraft, Concorde, jointly built by the British Aircraft Corporation and Aerospatiale at Toulouse. A total of ten Concordes – three for development purposes and seven for commercial service – were built at Filton.

Concorde 002 was the first supersonic aircraft to fly from Filton. It made its maiden flight on 9 April 1969. The subsonic flight from Filton to RAF Fairford, Gloucestershire, took twenty-two minutes. Afterwards Captain Brian Trubshaw, British Aircraft Corporation's Chief Test Pilot, who was at the controls, told waiting reporters: 'She flew like a bird.'

The last Concorde built at Filton, Concorde 216, made its final flight in November 2003. Flying from Heathrow it flew over Bristol, making a low flypast over the Clifton Suspension Bridge, before returning to its birthplace at Filton. It has stood there in the open air ever since while plans for a Concorde museum are discussed.

Filton Airfield closed in December 2012, bringing to an end 102 years of flying operations at Britain's s oldest continuously operating civil airfield. It was sold for redevelopment.

BRISTOL'S OWN CAR

After the Second World War, Bristol Aeroplane Company set up a motor car division to make use of the mechanical and aerodynamic skill its workforce had built up. The result was the hand-built luxury Bristol 400, a four-seater saloon that cost £2,724 in 1948. That year the car took third place in the Monte Carlo rally and was the first British car to finish. Bristol Cars, a subsidiary of the Bristol Aeroplane Company for fifteen years, made a limited number of saloons each year.

GETTING IT WRAPPED UP

Elisha Smith Robinson was probably the first person to make paper bags for resale when he went into business in 1844 in Redcliffe Street. Four years later his brother Alfred joined him and the firm traded as E.S. & A. Robinson, which eventually had factories across Bristol. In 1966 the printing, packaging and paper firm merged with another stationery company to form the Dickinson Robinson Group.

St Anne's Board Mills started making paperboard at its factory on the banks of the River Avon at St Anne's in 1914. At its peak the firm employed 4,000 people. The board mills closed in 1980 for economic reasons.

CREAM OF THE WINE TRADE

John Harvey & Sons of Bristol was one of the oldest wine firms in the world, having been founded in 1796. It started as a small family wine merchant selling mainly Spanish and Portuguese wines, including port and sherry. In the nineteenth century, John Harvey created a new blend of sherry that was called Harvey's Bristol Cream.

The original John Harvey came from a seafaring family but he himself got seasick. So he joined the wine firm he eventually took over to stay on dry land. From a Harvey's advertisement:

> Bristol Cream Sherry was blended in Harvey's cellars in Denmark Street in the centre of the city. It was here in 1882 that a lady was sampling the different sherries when she was offered Bristol Milk and then another finer blend. 'If this is Bristol Milk,' she said, 'then this must be the cream.' So it was then that Harvey's adopted the name for the sherry that Harvey's exported to 120 countries.

Harvey's was eventually swallowed up by a conglomerate that ultimately closed down the wine merchant in Bristol.

In his speech at the luncheon after he cut the first sod of earth at the Royal Edward Dock at Avonmouth in 1902, the Prince of Wales said: 'Lord Macaulay has told us of the splendour of the city, of its wealth, and its hospitality. He has given historical fame to Bristol Milk, that excellent wine with which today you have tempted us, under the still more potent title of Bristol Cream.'

The last Bristol Cream Sherry to be bottled in the city was in 1989.

Bristol Cream was selected for use on the Royal Train during the Indian tour of the Prince of Wales. The prince (later Edward VII) on tasting Bristol Milk, said: 'All I can say is that you must have some damn fine cows.'

LOTS OF BOTTLE

The oldest wine company in Bristol was J.R. Phillips, set up by William George in 1739. At one time the firm used the cellars underneath the Colston Hall – thought to be some of the oldest in the city and once used by monks – to keep its wine. Phillips closed its depot at Avonmouth in 1991.

Avery's wines set up business in 1793 and takes over the mantle of being the city's oldest surviving wine merchant with cellars beneath Park Street.

More than 1,000 different wines from nearly thirty countries were featured in the first World Wine Fair in July 1978. It was staged in disused dockside custom sheds and temporary pavilions and marquees erected around the City Docks. A touch of Venice was brought to the occasion with the creation of a mock Rialoto Bridge spanning St Augustine's Reach. The ten-day fair attracted 80,000 visitors and took place annually until 1992 but not always on such a grand scale.

The biggest wine warehouse in Europe can be found on a trading estate at Avonmouth. It holds 57 million bottles of wine. That's enough to fill fifteen Olympic-size swimming pools or if the bottles were laid end to end they would stretch 9,000 miles.

MINE'S A PINT

The biggest brewery in Bristol, Georges & Company, was established in the 1770s. A century later its directors issued a prospectus for the Bristol Brewery, Georges & Company to go public. They planned on keeping the share subscription list open for a week. However, the amount of £400,000 asked for was oversubscribed on the first day with the public offering £6,300,000. Georges not only brewed beer, but owned pubs and took over other breweries. In 1960 Georges itself was acquired by Courage, a national brewer which closed the Bristol Brewery site in 1999.

THE ENTREPRENEURIAL SPIRIT

John James, a docker's son from Bedminster, was regarded as one of the country's most successful post-war businessmen. He opened his first radio shop in Regent Street, Kingswood, with his Royal Air Force gratuity of £100. Within a year he had branches across the city. By 1958 he owned a radio and television chain with 300 stores, which he sold for £6 million. John James then started a chain of furniture stores, which he sold in 1979 for £25 million. James, who died in 1996 aged 89, was also a benefactor, supporting many local good causes.

A group of schoolmasters who had difficulty in obtaining books and academic papers for their schools, formed their own stationery company in 1870. The nine teachers, along with an accountant, called their business Scholastic Trading Company. In 1955 the firm opened its first shop in the centre of Bristol. Although the original intention was to supply only schools, the firm widened its interests and became stationers to many firms.

With capital of £140, Joyce Ley opened a cake shop in Princess Victoria Street, Clifton, in 1931 that she named 'Caroline's Cakes'. It was so successful that Mrs Ley went on to open a chain of cake shops across the city and ran three bakeries to supply them.

Using only handtools, presses and glues, in just six months in 1947 Martin Bailey single-handedly built a touring caravan in his workshop. Today Bailey Caravans occupy a 15-acre site at Bedminster Down and manufacture more than 7,000 caravans and motorhomes a year. One of their best-known customers is the former Foreign Secretary, Margaret Beckett and her husband who have bought four caravans.

FINANCIAL AFFAIRS

The first bank in the city opened in Corn Street in 1750, simply calling itself the Bristol Bank. After another bank set itself up in Bristol two years later the Bristol Bank became known as the Old Bank. By 1811 there were thirteen banks in the city and, unlike today, they were all allowed to print their own bank notes.

Bristol's importance as a financial and business centre was recognised when the Bank of England opened a branch near Bristol Bridge in 1827. Its manager was known as The Agent.

A group of local businessmen created the Bristol and West Building Society at a meeting in Bush Chambers, Corn Street, in 1850. The society quickly built up assets exceeding £2 million and had branches in most of the larger West Country towns. By the 1990s, when the society employed 1,206 people, it had assets of more than £2,256 million. In 1997 Bristol and West was taken over by the Bank of Ireland.

THE CITY'S OWN CURRENCY

The Bristol Pound (£B1), which was introduced in September 2012, is the UK's first citywide local currency. Nearly 1,000 businesses accept the Bristol Pound, which has equal value with £1 sterling. Bristolians can also pay local taxes with the new currency, including their Council Tax. When the scheme was announced, the city's directly elected mayor, George Ferguson, said that he would have his salary paid in Bristol Pounds.

The Bristol Pound is run as a not-for-profit social enterprise between the Bristol Pound Community Interest Company and Bristol Credit Union.

SIX FIRMS 'ONE HUNDRED NOT OUT'

Robert Patterson started an ironmongery business on Redcliffe Hill in 1889 that is still running more than 100 years later. Today Patterson's has not only grown into a major supplier of cleaning goods and pub trade equipment, but has also moved into much larger premises from where it runs a retail shop. Five members of the Patterson family are still involved with the company. One is the chairman and another is the longest-serving member of staff, having clocked up forty-one years.

Joseph Coleman set up his own building and decorating business when he was 25 years old with a contract to paint a row of houses. More than 120 years later Coleman's, who are based in Hotwells, has become one of the Bristol area's leading building firms. Although the family link ended in 1967, the firm still trades under its original name.

Building contractor Bray and Slaughter was founded in 1900 when Sydney Slaughter teamed up with Percy Bray who had a small plumbing business. The firm has always been based in south Bristol and has been at its present site in Bedminster since the 1950s.

The staff of Mogford's traditional ironmongery store in High Street, Westbury-on-Trym, can trace the history of the business back to 1850.

Samuel Veal started in business in 1846, selling guns and fishing tackle on Tower Hill. The firm traded here for 130 years before moving to nearby Old Market Street. After the Second World War, Veal's concentrated on selling solely fishing tackle. The firm now trades from Broad Plain.

Guilbert's chocolate company was founded in 1910 when Piers Guilbert, a young Swiss-Belgian, started making confectionery in a shop on Park Street. The firm may have had a number of different owners since then but the chocolates are still made to Mr Guilbert's recipe. Each one is handmade and hand-dipped. The chocolates are sold by some of the top London stores as well as shops in Bristol. Guilbert's is still privately owned and now makes chocolate in Small Street, a few doors away from where Joseph Fry started his chocolate firm in the eighteenth century.

WORKING UNDERGROUND

More than 3,000 men were working in the city's collieries in 1909. They were producing about 500,000 tons of coal a year. The last colliery to mine coal was the South Liberty Lane pit at Ashton Vale, which was closed in 1925.

Miners at South Liberty Lane Colliery were paid 7½*d* for each ton of coal they dug. If they were lucky they might dig out 70 tons of coal a week. Boys who pushed drams or led pit ponies were paid 15*s* a week. When there were rockfalls miners could spend several days clearing away the debris without being paid.

Fifty miners were buried down the pit at the Malago Colliery on 20 June 1851 but remarkably they were all rescued alive and well forty hours later.

At the Dean Lane pit in Southville eight men lost their lives in an explosion on 10 September 1887. It was thought they were killed by a gas known as 'after damp'. Colliery explosions were not uncommon. Unlike today, however, many of the mining tragedies received scant coverage in the newspapers; often it was just a paragraph when the coroner's report was published many months later.

RETAIL THERAPY

Bristol's first supermarket had its roots in a small grocery shop that James Harding Mills opened on Redcliffe Hill in 1875, stocking everything from Bristol-made soap to candles. By the 1950s J.H. Mills & Company had more than a dozen branches across the city and were taken over by the Bristol-based Tyndall Group. The shops were renamed Gateway. In turn they became supermarkets, with the first one opening in 1958.

When Gateway (the name has long-disappeared) arrived in Clifton Village in 1959, the local newspapers reported one resident as saying: 'We don't want one of those dreadful supermarkets here.' Another said the store would 'spoil the atmosphere of Clifton'. Someone else protested that 'price-cutting by supermarkets was rather vulgar'.

Alexandra's department store in Whiteladies Road, Clifton, reported on 4 January 1955 what it described as 'the biggest sales rush of its history'. The manager put the number of customers in the store at any one time in the morning at 1,500. Customers often took away their purchases unwrapped to ease the burden of the sales girls. Shoppers were attracted by the main offer of nylon stockings at 2s 11d a pair. By midday 2,800 pairs had been sold.

It was estimated that on the first day of trading 100,000 people swarmed through the 200 departments on the eight floors of Lewis's departmental store, which had cost £3 million to build. Some 3,000 people applied for the 800 jobs on offer when the store opened in The Horsefair in 1957. Lewis's sold out in a £7 million deal in 1980 to the John Lewis Partnership, a totally different company with a totally different name.

Many thousands of shoppers turned up for the opening day of the £500 million Cabot Circus retail and leisure complex on the edge of Broadmead in September 2008. More than 4,000 jobs were created with the opening of the complex, which had taken ten years to plan and build.

Cabot Circus was not its original name. The developers wanted to call it Merchants' Quarter but that name came under fire because of its association with the slave trade. Cabot Circus was chosen after a public vote.

The four-storey complex has 140 shops, two department stores, a thirteen-screen cinema, hotel, restaurants and 200 apartments. The tenants pay more than £17 million a year to the landowners. Cabot Circus attracts more than 18 million people a year and has 2,500 car park spaces.

BUSINESSMEN'S CLUBS

Clubs where businessmen could read the London newspapers and discuss affairs of the day with their colleagues over coffee were popular in the nineteenth and twentieth centuries. Bristol's first such club – and it went on to be the oldest – was the Commercial Rooms which opened in Corn Street in 1811. Its first president was John Loudon McAdam, inventor of the tar macadam road surface, who was living in Clifton at the time. In the early part of the nineteenth century he was general surveyor of roads for the Bristol Turnpike Trust.

A dial on one of the club's walls was connected to a weathervane. It told businessmen when winds were favourable for their ships carrying cargos to make their way through the Avon Gorge into the City Docks.

The Commercial Rooms had a record membership of 1,056 in 1920 but towards the end of the twentieth century it had dwindled so much that the club closed in 1995 and was bought by a national pub company. It spent £1 million refurbishing the Georgian building but retained many of the club's original features including the wind vane and the club's name. There were two other similar businessmen's clubs nearby, the Bristol Club and the Constitutional Club, both of which also closed about the same time.

BUSINESS BULLETIN

The royal phone call

There was a communications boost for businesses in December 1958 thanks to a phone call the queen made from Bristol. Her Majesty was in the city to inaugurate Subscriber Trunk Dialling from Bristol's central telephone exchange. This meant that telephone subscribers could now make trunk calls without the help of an operator. Her Majesty dialled the Lord Provost of Edinburgh and during a two-minute call said: 'This is the queen speaking from Bristol. Good afternoon Lord Provost.' In an equally formal and stilted reply he said: 'Good afternoon Your Majesty. May I, with humble duty, offer you the loyal greetings of the City of Edinburgh.'

Traders tax protest

Most of the retailers in the city closed their businesses for one day in 1785 as a protest against the Chancellor of the Exchequer's imposition of a tax on shops. In the protest, shop windows were decorated with emblems of mourning and church bells rang muffled peals. The chancellor abolished the tax four years later.

Street fairs and markets

Fairs played an important part in a trader's life in Victorian times with many street markets being held in the centre of the city. Besides this a Colt Fair was held at the Cattle Market in July, and Leather Fairs at The Exchange, Corn Street, in March and September alongside a Wool Fair. A Hide Market was held in what is now the Fleece and Firkin music pub in St Thomas Street and a Cheese Market was held in Union Street twice a week.

Cash only, please

An unusual advert appeared on the front page of the first edition of the *Western Daily Press* in 1858. It was placed by a family grocer, Edward Bonser, who traded from a shop in Union Street, Broadmead. In the advert he told prospective customers that he would be 'selling only and exclusively for cash'. He said he had adopted this principle because 'several millions of pounds sterling are annually lost in England alone by bad debts'.

TRADING NAMES
LONG DISAPPEARED FROM BRISTOL

The **Ashton Court Country Club** was a leisure and sports club at Failand on the Somerset side of the Clifton Suspension Bridge that opened in the early 1960s.

The **Assize Courts Hotel** was a city-centre hotel close to the law courts. It is now a restaurant.

Berni Inns was a steak and chips restaurant chain that began in Bristol but quickly expanded nationally.

Bristol Commercial Vehicles made buses and trucks at Brislington.

Bristol Illustrated News was a monthly 'county'-style magazine covering 'society' events.

Bristol United Brewery had its headquarters and brewery in Lewins Mead. The brewery merged with George's Brewery which itself was later taken over.

Bristol Omnibus Company was a citywide bus operator.

Bristol Siddeley Engines Ltd made aircraft engines at Patchway.

Clark's Grammar School was a private school in Clifton.

G.B. Britton made boots and shoes at its Kingswood factory.

Broadmead Radio was a citywide chain of radio and television shops started by self-made businessman John James who used his fortune for charitable works.

H.W. Carter was a soft drinks manufacturer which invented Ribena.

Frost & Reed an art dealer established in the reign of George III.

Godwin Warren Engineering advertised itself as the largest steel stockholder in the West Country.

The **Great Western Cotton Factory,** which was founded at Barton Hill in 1838, once employed 1,500 people. It ceased trading in 1925.

The **Great Western Railway Company.**

The **Grosvenor Hotel** stood close to Temple Meads railway station.

The **House of Lewis Ltd,** founded on College Green in 1946, described itself as 'Naval, military, RAF and Mufti tailors'.

Lennards opened their first shoe shop in High Street in 1877 and eventually expanded to 175 branches nationally.

Llewellins and James, bell founders, Castle Green.

The **Little Theatre** was a small theatre inside the Colston Hall that ran from the early 1920s to the 1960s.

Lowell Baldwin & Company was a citywide firm of coal merchants.

John Lysaght and Company, a galvanised metal maker founded in 1857, was taken over in 1920 and its name disappeared.

Mardon, Son and Hall, founded in Bristol in 1823, printed cigarette cards and made card and packaging.

T.C. Marsh Ltd were tailors and outfitters 'by appointment' to Bristol University and more than 100 schools, clubs and colleges.

May & Hassell, a timber importer, was based in the City Docks.

Peckett & Sons Ltd built locomotive tanks at its factory in St George.

St Vincent's Rocks Hotel stood opposite Clifton Suspension Bridge. It is now private residential accommodation.

Tratman and Lowther was a firm of ships stores merchants and sail makers founded in 1812 by two Bristol brothers.

Verrecchias's sold its homemade ice cream in its own ice cream parlours across the city as well as selling it from its fleet of vans that toured the suburbs.

W.J. Rogers was a brewery in Jacob Street, Old Market.

HOW TO GET THE PRODUCT KNOWN

Advertising slogans are nothing new. In 1879 the Wilsonia Depot in Boyce's Avenue, Clifton, which sold magnetic belts, corsets, vests and gloves, were using the following memorable lines on their advertising cards:

'Take medicine and die,
Apply magnetic currents and live.'

8

THE WORLD OF ENTERTAINMENT

THE CITY'S EARLY THEATRES

John Hippisley, a popular actor from London, built one of Bristol's first theatres in 1729. He chose a site on what is now Jacobs Wells Road in Hotwells. His theatre attracted many theatrical companies from London with their productions. The theatre opened with Congreve's *Love for Love*.

The stage was so small that actors moving from one side to the other had to go outside, run around the building and hopefully get back on stage in time for their cues. Crowds of people gathered on Brandon Hill Park opposite to see the actors in their costumes.

A strange feature of the theatre was a hole in the wall that allowed members of the audience to place their orders for drinks with the pub next door.

Hippisley's theatre closed shortly after another theatre, later to be known as the Theatre Royal, opened in King Street in 1766. It is now the oldest – although not continuous – working theatre in the country. Protests from churches and other organisations meant that the first play was staged under the disguise of it being 'a concert of music' and 'a specimen of rhetoric'. It was another two years before the theatre was called 'Royal'.

Fifty supporters each pledged £50 toward the cost of building the Theatre Royal. In return they were given a silver token each numbered from one to fifty. The tokens entitled the holders to 'the sight of every performance to be exhibited in this house'. If you should be fortunate enough to come into possession of one it is still valid.

The Theatre Royal is often mistakenly called the 'Old Vic', which is a contraction of the Bristol Old Vic Theatre Company. This was formed in 1946 as an offshoot of the London Old Vic. It was the first resident company of actors in the Theatre Royal's history.

The new company set up the Bristol Old Vic Theatre School, which was affectionately known as the 'fruit school'. It was housed in a building near the theatre's stage door that was surrounded by the city's fruit and vegetable markets. The school was officially opened by the renowned actor, Sir Laurence Olivier.

Ten years later in 1956 the school moved in to two large Victorian houses on the edge of Clifton Downs, its present home. Many of its graduates have become household names. They include:

Helen Baxendale	Aled Jones
Stephanie Cole	Peter Postlethwaite
Sir Daniel Day-Lewis	Jenny Seagrove
Alex Jennings	Samantha Bond
Tim Piggott-Smith	Jeremy Irons
Miranda Richardson	Jane Lapotaire
Greta Scacchi	Patricia Routledge
Brian Blessed	

The Princes Theatre

A real-life drama happened at the Princes Theatre, Park Row, on Boxing Day 1869 when fourteen people were crushed to death and twenty others injured at the theatre's entrance. It happened when the doors opened for the *Robinson Crusoe* pantomime and theatregoers surged down a slope at the side of the building. Some of them fell while others unknowingly walked over them. In true theatrical tradition the show went on with the audience being told of the disaster only when the final curtain came down.

Bristol Hippodrome

The city's biggest theatre, the Hippodrome, opened in December 1912 and since then has hosted some of the most famous ballet troupes, orchestras, operas and comedy acts. The theatre's opening night production was an aqua-drama called *Sands O'Dee*. It was based on verses written by West Country clergyman the Revd Charles Kingsley who also wrote novels and poems.

Underneath the Hippodrome's stage was a specially built tank that held 100,000 gallons of water that could be heated up to a temperature of 80°. The tank had a hydraulically controlled moving base that was designed to create waves. It came into its own in the *Sands O'Dee* when the hero of the production galloped on horseback through the water. A glass screen that could be raised in front of the tank at the touch of a lever saved the orchestra and the audience, especially those in the front row, from being splashed by water.

The Hippodrome's management claimed that 'there is not another stage so constructed in the world'.

A dome in the roof, which can be slid open at will to reveal the sky and let in fresh air, is still in place, unlike the water tank.

When the Hippodrome opened, the theatre's management claimed that it could accommodate more than 3,000 people. Anyone finding the standing room too crowded could get a refund.

Within its first year the Hippodrome had hosted the famous French actress Sarah Bernhardt and her company, which performed the fifth act of *La Dame aux Camellias* and was at the theatre for a week.

More than 4,000 shows have been staged at the Hippodrome with 30,000 artists taking part. Those who have 'trod the boards' at the theatre include Rudolf Nureyev and Margot Fonteyn, John Gielgud, Peter Sellers, Frank Sinatra, Marlene Dietrich, Tom Jones, and the D'Oyle Carte opera company.

Four of the many premieres staged at The Hippodrome
1953 – The British premiere of *Guys and Dolls*
        starring Sam Levene and Stubby Kaye.
1961 – The European premiere of *The Music Man*
        starring Van Johnson.
1982 – The world premiere of *Windy City*
        starring Dennis Waterman and Anita Rodgers.
2004 – The world premiere of *Mary Poppins*.

Backstage blaze
Fire caused extensive damage to the Hippodrome's stage and the area behind it in 1948. The blaze was probably caused by a discarded cigarette stub or match. It meant the theatre was closed for ten months for repairs to the stage and refurbishment of areas that were smoke-damaged. The Hippodrome reopened on Christmas Eve with the pantomime *Cinderella*. However, the curtain refused to fully rise so comedian Ted Ray, who was playing the part of Buttons, went out in front of it and ad-libbed for thirty minutes while repairs were carried out.

Vows take centre stage
Many weddings have taken place on the Hippodrome's stage as part of various productions. But on 25 July 2014 the first real-life wedding took place on the stage when magician and entertainer Chris Cox tied the knot with his bride Helen Lagunowitsch. Instead of a paying audience in the stalls the seats were taken up by the families and friends of the bridal couple.

MUSICAL NOTES

Colston Hall: A concert hall for the city
A major concert venue for the city, Colston Hall was opened in 1867.
It was built on the site of a thirteenth-century Carmelite friary that later
became Colston Boys' School. The concert hall initially cost £17,000
but with additions over the next fifteen years the bill totalled £40,000.

Fires destroy Colston Hall
A fire that spread from a next-door clothing factory in 1898 destroyed
the hall and its organ leaving just its walls standing. Colston Hall was
rebuilt and reopened three years later.

   Disaster struck the hall again when a fire started by a discarded
cigarette stub destroyed it in 1945. More than 100 firefighters were
needed to put out the blaze. Colston Hall was rebuilt and reopened in
1951 in time for the Festival of Britain celebrations which were taking
place all over the country.

The Beatles at Colston Hall

The Beatles made the first of three appearances in Bristol at Colston Hall in March 1963. They were then a support act to the American singers Tommy Roe and Chris Montez. The Beatles sang six of their own numbers.

In November 1963 the 'Fab Four' from Liverpool – as they were now being called by newspapers – returned to Colston Hall. This time fans of The Beatles got a better deal, for the foursome sang ten of their own numbers.

There were dramatic scenes when The Beatles topped the bill on their third appearance at Colston Hall in November 1964. While the group was playing 'If I Fell', several pranksters who had found their way into the building's loft, despite tight security, dropped a bag of flour on to the stage 50ft below. The Beatles, who were covered in white flour, simply laughed and played on. It was the last night of their UK tour and 2,000 fans had packed the hall. It has never been discovered who was responsible for the flour prank.

Colston Hall becomes a private club for controversial musical

The curtain went up in 1960 on a church youth club production of *A Man Dies*, a modern version of Christ's Passion which was set to rock 'n' roll music. It was co-written by the Revd Ernest Marvin of St James church, Lockleaze, and had Jesus wearing jeans and talking slang. The play became controversial with critics, including Members of Parliament, who claimed it was blasphemous and called for it to be banned.

The musical was later staged at Colston Hall, which had become a *private* club especially for the occasion. This got around a ruling by the Lord Chancellor who had refused to licence any *public* portrayal of Jesus Christ on stage. Members of the public wanting to see *A Man Dies* had to join the newly formed St James Theatre Club to buy a ticket. The musical was also staged at the Royal Albert Hall and broadcast on television.

A patient pop fan

When the Colston Hall box office opened to sell tickets for a concert by the Bay City Rollers pop group in 1975 the first person in the queue was a 16-year-old girl from London. She had been waiting outside the hall for two days although she had already seen the Bay City Rollers in several other towns.

Pop goes school career

Two 15-year-old boarders were expelled from school in 1971 for attending a concert at Colston Hall without permission. They had seen the 'progressive pop' band Quintessence. The *Bristol Evening Post* reported headmistress Miss Clare Harvey as saying: 'I have no comment to make. This is just a question of school discipline.' The management of Colston Hall banned Quintessence from appearing there again because they had given burning joss sticks to the audience.

MUSICAL FIRSTS

The world premiere of composer Ralph Vaughan Williams' work 'The Lark Ascending' was staged at Shirehampton Public Hall in 1920. This particular suburban venue was chosen as Vaughan Williams regularly visited nearby Kings Weston House where his friend, Napier Miles, who conducted a local choral society, lived.

Vaughan Williams started writing 'The Lark Ascending' before the First World War but his musical activities came to a temporary halt when he joined the army. He revised his work after the war ended and staged its premiere in conjunction with Avonmouth and Shirehampton Choral Society. Today 'The Lark Ascending' is frequently voted by music-lovers as their favourite classical work.

The composer Robert Pearsall (1795–1856), who was born at Clifton, had such a musical talent that by the age of 13 he had written a cantata. Entitled 'Saul and the Witch of Endor' it was printed privately. Pearsall eventually devoted himself to composing madrigals. Much of his work was performed by the Bristol Madrigal Society of which he was one of the first members. He died suddenly of a stroke.

The first performance in Bristol of Handel's 'Messiah' took place in St Paul's church in Portland Square in April 1803. It was performed by a 120-strong orchestra and choir at a 'grand musical festival' that raised funds for the Bristol Infirmary.

A 'MUSICAL' WINDOW

A window in the north choir aisle of St Mary Redcliffe has eight passages from Handel's 'Messiah' etched into it. Handel was a friend of the Revd Thomas Broughton, Redcliffe's vicar from 1744–74. It is often said that Handel revised some of his oratorios on the church's organ although there is no documentary evidence to support this theory. However, Mr Broughton did write the words for some of Handel's compositions, including the musical drama 'Hercules', which had its premiere in London in 1745.

ROCK 'N' ROLL'S LOSS

The Hippodrome staged what turned out to be the last-ever performance by the American rock 'n' roll singer Eddie Cochrane in April 1960. It was the last night of his UK tour and he sang one of his most popular numbers 'Three Steps to Heaven'. After the show, Cochrane was being driven back to Heathrow Airport when his taxi hit a lamppost in Chippenham. The 21-year-old-singer was taken to hospital in Bath where he died from head injuries. Also in the car were Cochrane's girlfriend, Sharon Sheeley, his tour manager Pat Thompkins and the taxi driver, George Martin. Fortunately, they escaped injury.

STARS SHINE AT THE GRAND SPA

Many rising pop stars of the 1960s, including Shirley Bassey and Petula Clark, made some of their early appearances at dance nights and pop concerts organised in the ballroom of the Grand Spa Hotel in Clifton.

THREE EARLY CONCERT SINGERS

Opera singer Jenny Lind, known as the 'Swedish Nightingale', gave several recitals in Bristol, one of them at a concert at the Victoria Rooms, Clifton. She also visited Clifton Hill House where it is said the pitch of her voice broke a crystal glass on the mantelpiece of a marble fireplace.

Bristol's best-known recitalist and concert singer was the contralto Dame Clara Butt. She came to the city with her family when she was aged 7 and started taking singing lessons. Clara Butt made several early gramophone records, the best known being her rendering of 'Land of Hope and Glory'. She eventually became a world performer and it was joked that her booming voice, with its amazing range and power, could be heard on the other side of the English Channel.

When Clara Butt married baritone Robert Kennerley Rumford at Bristol Cathedral in 1900, many employers closed their shops, offices and factories so their staff could see the wedding. Clara Butt was given a diamond and ruby brooch that had been bought by the people of Bristol. It was engraved with the initials 'CB' which could mean either Clara Butt or City of Bristol.

Ruby Holder (1890–1938), who was promoted as Bristol's first female tenor, grew up with her parents at their pub in Lawrence Hill. After her voice was spotted and trained, Ruby made her debut at Queen's Hall, London, in 1913. Her fame later took her around the world performing at some of the world's best-known concert halls.

BRISTOL'S GOT TALENT

Randolph Sutton (1888–1969), who was born near Clifton Down, became known as Britain's premiere light comedian. He was a popular stage and music hall entertainer for several decades. Sutton gave his songs catchy titles like 'Mrs Rush and Her Scrubbing Brush' and 'Where Do The Jam Jars Go?' One of his most popular numbers was 'On Mother Kelly's Doorstep'. Sutton began his singing career as a chorister at his local church.

Singer Rosemary Squires, who was born at Kingsdown, had her first radio series in 1949 and has not been out of the showbiz spotlight ever since. In the early days of her career she shared top billing with many well-known artistes including Danny Kaye, Sammy Davis Jr, Cliff Richard and Ken Dodd. Rosemary Squires is also known for the jingles she has recorded for television commercials, including the longest-running one of all time, 'Now hands that do dishes can feel soft as your face with mild green Fairy Liquid'. Rosemary, who now lives in Wiltshire, has been in show business for sixty years. However, she shows no signs of retiring, being in demand to sing at clubs from Cumbria to Cornwall.

Trevor Stanford, who achieved fame in the 1950s and '60s as honky-tonk pianist Russ Conway, was born in Coronation Road, Southville. His playing style and his own compositions twice took him to the number one spot in the pop record charts with 'Side Saddle' and 'Roulette'. During more than forty years in show business Russ Conway sold more than 30 million records. He was in the UK singles charts for a total of eighty-three weeks between 1957–63. Russ Conway died in 2000 and at his request 'Side Saddle' was played at the end of his funeral service.

Acker Bilk had the honour of being the first British artist to have a record at the number one spot in the American Bill Board Hot 100. This was his own tune 'Stranger on the Shore', which hit the American top spot in May 1962. Bilk, who was born at Pensford near Bristol in 1929, originally wrote the piece for his daughter but it was later used as the theme tune of a BBC TV series of the same name. At the peak of his career Acker, who has played the clarinet all over the world, often turned up unannounced at jazz pubs in Bristol and played.

The internationally famous modern jazz player and composer Andy Sheppard was born in Bristol in 1956 and educated in the city. He is self-taught, having taken up the saxophone when he was aged 19. Sheppard now plays with leading jazz and classical groups all over the world.

Adge Cutler wrote songs about Somerset villages and Bristol suburbs that he sang with his so-called Scrumpy and Western group, The Wurzels. In 1976 The Wurzels reached the top of the record charts with 'Combine Harvester'. Unfortunately, Adge had died two years earlier, aged 44, in a car crash while driving home after playing at a concert in Hereford.

Catherine Johnson has never stood in front of the footlights but she still deserves a mention. As a playwright and screenwriter, Catherine, who once lived in Hotwells, is best known for writing the script of the West End Abba musical *Mamma Mia!* She also wrote the screenplay for the film of the same name.

THERE'S NO BUSINESS LIKE SHOW BUSINESS

John Miles started his career in show business by managing local pop groups and booking gigs for them in village halls. At one time he had around 300 groups on his books and ran the operation from a small office in Whiteladies Road, Clifton. More than fifty years on he has sole representation for some of the best-known names in the entertainment industry, including Carol Vorderman, Noel Edmonds, Des O'Connor and Timmy Mallet. The small office has been swapped for an administrative suite that is part of John's home in the countryside near Bristol.

THE BRISTOL FILM FILE

Bristol has long been a favourite location for film producers and location managers. In 1962 Bristol South Swimming Baths doubled up as a roller-skating rink after the pool was boarded over for the filming of *Some People*. This was a promotional feature film for the Duke of Edinburgh's Award Scheme starring Kenneth More, Angela Douglas, Harry H. Corbett in his pre-Harold Steptoe days, and David Hemmings. It was filmed entirely in and around Bristol. Locations included the Palace Hotel, Old Market, Bristol Hippodrome, the Magnet Fish and Chip shop in Southville and Fry's chocolate factory at Somerdale, Keynsham.

The Ostrich pub on the edge of Bathurst Basin was one of the locations for the 1964 film *Beauty Jungle*. The pub then had the reputation of being a cider house with footprints painted on the ceiling and old bus seats providing accommodation. The film, as its title might suggest, was about the life of a beauty queen and starred Janette Scott and Ian Hendry.

A Day in the Death of Joe Egg, shot in 1972, was an adaptation of Bristol playwright Peter Nichol's account of a young family coping with a severely disabled child. The film cameras were seen in Freeland Place, Hotwells, parts of Clifton and Broadmead shopping centre. Appearing before the cameras were the actors Alan Bates, Janet Suzman and Peter Bowles.

The Medusa Touch brought screen stars Richard Burton and Lee Remick to the city in 1978. In the film Bristol Cathedral became a substitute for Westminster Cathedral. This psychological thriller was about a man who causes disasters just by thinking about them.

Hearts of Fire was a musical film drama that was shot in America and England in 1987. The concert scenes starring rock star Bob Dylan were filmed in the Colston Hall with some of his fans hired as 'extras' to play the audience. The storyline followed a would-be pop star who arrived in England with Bob Dylan to record her debut album.

Paper Mask was a medical thriller filmed around Clifton and Durdham Downs, Clifton Suspension Bridge and the former Bristol General Hospital in 1990. Cheddar Gorge in Somerset, and Hammersmith, London, were other locations. The cast list included Amanda Donohoe, Barbara Leigh-Hunt and Paul McGann, who lives in Bristol.

King Street, in the middle of the city, doubled up as Soho for the producers of *In These Foolish Things*. This drama-cum-comedy was set in London in the 1930s. The film, made in 2004, starred Lauren Bacall and Angelica Huston.

The Truth About Love, a romantic comedy, saw Jennifer Love Hewitt bringing a touch of Hollywood stardust to Clifton where some of the film was shot. The Paragon and Royal York Crescent appear in some of the scenes. Redcliffe Wharf, Merchants' Quay and Severnshed restaurant were also used as locations. Ms Hewitt was joined by Dougray Scott and Jimi Mistry in the main roles of the film, which was made in 2007.

Starter for Ten, which was filmed in 2006, was a drama/comedy which followed the life of a first-year student determined to appear on *University Challenge*. In the film, Bristol University students' union building in Queens Road became a chemistry school. Christmas Steps, Redcliffe Wharf and Royal York Crescent were also used for some of the settings. The film starred James McAvoy and James Gordon. It was an adaptation of a book of the same title by David Nicholls, a graduate of Bristol University.

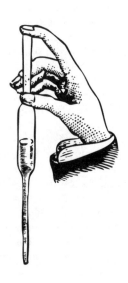

THE CITY'S OWN HOLLYWOOD STAR

Archibald Leach, who was born in Hughenden Road, Horfield, in 1904 became better known as Cary Grant. He went to the local Bishop Road Primary School and from the age of 11 he attended Fairfield Grammar School from which he was expelled at the age of 14. He joined a troupe of acrobats but Hollywood quickly beckoned.

Cary Grant became a great screen lover and comic actor. During his film career he made seventy-four films, the last being in 1966 when he retired, having acted with screen stars including Dietrich, Bergman and Hepburn. His films include *Arsenic and Old Lace*, *North By Northwest*, *Philadelphia Story* and *Bringing Up Baby*.

Despite his fame Grant never severed his links with his native city. He brought each of his five wives home to meet his mother, who was in a nursing home.

Cary Grant died in 1986 aged 82. However, the city of his birth was rather slow in recognising his fame. It wasn't until 2001 that a statue of the star was installed in Millennium Square.

Bristol now has the largest dedicated film and television studio in the West of England in a former winery and bottling plant at Hengrove. It once housed the production line for bottling Harvey's Bristol Cream Sherry. The building, now known as Bottle Yard Studios, is the production base for films including *Wolf Hall*, a BBC2 adaption of the Booker Prize-winning novels, and the BBC1 drama *Poldark*. The studios also host Noel Edmonds' Channel 4 game show *Deal or No Deal*.

CINEMAS THAT NO LONGER EXIST

1908 The Bio Pictureland, Counterslip
1909 The Gem, Broadweir
      The Town Hall Cinema, Cannon Street, Bedminster
      Vestry Hall, Pennywell Road, Easton
1910 The Olympia, Carey's Lane, Old Market
      Dolphin Picture House, Dolphin Street (now Castle Park)
1911 The Park Picture House, St George
      Clare Picture House, Clare Street, city centre
      His Majesty's, Stapleton Road
      The King's, Old Market
1912 The Coliseum, Park Row
      People's Palace (later the Gaumont Cinema)
      Baldwin Street, City Centre
      The Regal, Staple Hill
1913 Hippodrome, Eastville
      The Metropole, Sussex Place, St Paul's
      The Knowle Picture House, Wells Road, Knowle
      Brislington Picture Hall, Sandy Park Road, Brislington
1914 The Magnet, Newfoundland Road, St Paul's
      The Plaza, Cheltenham Road
      Premier, Gloucester Road
      The Plaza, North Street, Ashton Gate
      Globe Cinema, Lawrence Hill
      Triangle, Clifton
1915 The Hippodrome, East Street, Bedminster
      Hotwells Cinema, Hotwells Road
1920 The Clifton Spa (this cinema was set up in the ballroom of
      the Grand Spa Hotel, Clifton, but was relatively short-lived)
1921 Whiteladies Picture House, Whiteladies Road, Clifton
1926 The Vandyck, Fishponds
1928 Kingsway, Two Mile Hill, St George
      The Regent, Castle Street (now Castle Park)
1933 Carlton Cinema and Cafe, Westbury-on-Trym
      The Gaiety, Wells Road, Knowle
      The News Theatre, Castle Street (now Castle Park)
      Embassy Super Cinema, Queen's Avenue, Clifton
      The Savoy, Shirehampton
1935 Cabot Cinema, Gloucester Road, Filton
1936 The Odeon, Winterstoke Road, Ashton Gate
1938 Broadway, Filwood Park
      The Ritz, Brislington

When the Duchess of Beaufort opened the Whiteladies Cinema in 1921 she was joined by the Archdeacon of Bristol. The management of the Whiteladies claimed at the time that the cinema had the largest auditorium in the West of England with 1,016 seats on the ground floor and a further 282 in the balcony. The Whiteladies Cinema also boasted a cafe and ballroom. Its last films were screened in 2000 – the management said it was no longer economic – and the cinema has remained closed ever since.

9

LITERARY BRISTOL

EARLY HISTORIES

An eighteenth-century surgeon is believed to have written the first history of the city. William Barrett researched his book by collecting records from the homes of families he visited and turning them into more than thirty chapters on the origins of Bristol up to its development in the eighteenth century. He published his book in 1789.

Lord Macaulay (1800–1859), best known for his books on British history, lived in Caledonia Place, Clifton. A plaque on the house marks the time he was there and also states that his mother was a Bristolian. Macaulay is best known for his *History of Britain* although he wrote many other books, essays and reviews.

John Latimer (1824–1904) came to Bristol from his native Newcastle-on-Tyne to be editor of the *Bristol Mercury*, a post he held for twenty-five years. He loved the city so much that he recorded its history in three hefty volumes. His *Annals of Bristol* begin in the seventeenth century and cover the events of 300 years, almost day by day.

BRISTOL BROUGHT TO BOOK

Writer and historian Philippa Gregory is well known for her books set in Tudor times. However, she also wrote *A Respectable Trade*, a controversial novel about the eighteenth-century slave trade in England that she based in Bristol. Although Gregory was born in Nairobi, she was brought up in the city and educated at Colston Girls' School.

Travel writer Celia Fiennes (1662–1741), who visited every county in England on horseback, wrote about Hotwells Spa in her book *Through England on a Side Saddle*. She described the waters as 'warm as new milk and much of the sweetness'.

In her novel *Evelina* the writer and diarist Fanny Burney (1752–1840) has her heroine describing Hotwells as: 'A most delightful spot; the prospect is beautiful, the air pure and the water very favourable to invalids.'

Author and poet Tobias Smollett set some of his novel *The Expedition of Humphry Clinker* in Hotwells at a time when its spa was attracting many visitors from all over Europe.

Jane Austen described Blaise Castle, 5 miles north-west of the city centre, as 'The finest place in England' in her novel *Northanger Abbey* which she wrote in 1804.

Hannah More who was born at Fishponds in 1745 went on to become one of the most influential writers and philanthropists of her time. She was one of the top-earning writers in eighteenth- and nineteenth-century England. Her plays, stories for children, religious tracts, a novel, poems and essays are estimated to have earned her £40,000. Hannah More gradually turned from writing to social reform, fighting poverty, ignorance and drink. She died in Clifton in 1833 aged 88.

Maria Edgeworth (1767–1849) who wrote witty and improving stories for children, some of them with a local setting, lived in Princes Buildings near the Clifton Suspension Bridge. She also wrote novels for adults, the best known of which was *Castle Rackrent*.

Clifton was thinly disguised as Upper Radstowe in seven of the novels that Emily Hilda Young wrote between 1922–47. Canynge Square, for example, became Chatterton Square. Young married a local lawyer and lived in Saville Place, Clifton.

In his novel *Pickwick Papers*, Charles Dickens had Mr Winkle lodging at the Bush Tavern in Corn Street during his lovelorn quest for the missing Arabella Allen. The pub, which was known for its lavish banquets, was demolished in 1858 to make way for the West of England and South Wales Bank that eventually went bankrupt.

Novelist Emma Marshall (1830–1899) came to Bristol in her late teens and later married a clergyman's son. She took to writing after the bank in which her husband worked crashed. Mrs Marshall wanted to make sure that the household bills could be paid through sales of her books. She wrote more than 100 romances, children's books and historical novels. Many of them were based on Bristol's history. The best known are *In Colston's Days*, *By the Sword Divided* and *Bristol Diamonds*.

Angela Carter (1940–1992) arrived in Bristol in 1959 as a student to read English at the university after working as a journalist in London. Her course triggered her career as a novelist, writing *Shadow Dance* and *The Magic Toyshop* while she lived in Clifton. One of her novels, *The Company of Wolves*, was turned into a film for which she wrote the screenplay.

Deborah Moggach, a student at Bristol University in the 1960s, used Clifton and Hotwells as backgrounds for her first novel *You Must Be Sisters*, which was published in 1978.

CONTEMPORARY LOCAL NOVELISTS

Bristol mental health nurse Nathan Filer won two major literary awards in 2014 for his first novel *The Shock of the Fall*. It charts a young man's descent into schizophrenia. Filer was awarded the Costa Book of the Year and the Costa First Novel awards.

Helen Dunmore, who was born in Yorkshire and taught for two years in Finland, now lives in Bristol. Having written her first novel, *Zennor in Darkness*, in 1993, she has since penned another thirteen books. Dunmore has also written a short story collection, books for children and young adults as well as a poetry collection. She has won prizes for both her poetry and prose.

On her own admission, Susan Lewis says that she worked hard at behaving badly while she was a boarder at Red Maids' School. Her aim was to be expelled – and she succeeded – because she wanted to return to the family home at Kingswood, which she missed. Susan Lewis's time at Red Maids' is recorded in her autobiographical memoir. It is one of thirty books she has now written, most of them in the chick-lit genre, which has made her one of Britain's top-selling authors.

Jill Mansell gave up her job as an electroencephalographic technician at the Burden Neurological Hospital to become a full-time novelist. Since her first book was published in 1991, Mansell, who lives in Stoke Bishop, has brought out almost thirty more. She is now listed amongst the bestselling chick-lit authors.

Ernest Thompson spent nine years as a policeman in Bristol Constabulary's newly formed vice squad in the 1950s before turning to a career as a writer. His experience of working in the city's slum areas was used in a series of books that he set in nineteenth-century Lewins Mead. Thompson (1931–2012) wrote more than forty novels and during his lifetime he sold some 4 million copies.

The late Terry Pratchett, author of the comic fantasy *Discworld* novels, was a journalist for the *Western Daily Press* and later worked in public relations in Bristol before writing books. His books have sold more than 40 million copies all over the world in both paperback and hardback.

Beverley Nichols (1898–1983) was a writer, playwright and magazine columnist who was born in Bower Ashton on the southern edge of Bristol. After his first book was published in 1920, Nichols wrote more than sixty books and plays over the next sixty-two years. They included novels, mysteries, short stories and children's books. He was also known for a column he wrote for *Woman's Own* magazine for more than twenty years. This was regarded as something of a record in the cut-throat world of Fleet Street.

PLAYWRIGHTS WITH LOCAL CONNECTIONS

Sir Tom Stoppard, born in 1937, began his writing career as a journalist, working for the *Western Daily Press* and the *Bristol Evening Post* before becoming one of Britain's best dramatists. He was born in Czechoslovakia and came to England when he was 9 years old. After his experience with the local newspapers he moved to London to freelance as a theatre critic and write plays for radio. Stoppard made his name as a playwright with *Rosencrantz and Guildenstern Are Dead*, which had its premiere at the Edinburgh Festival in 1966. He has written numerous plays, which have been performed around the world.

Novelist and playwright Iris Murdoch (1919–1999) was educated at Badminton School, Westbury-on-Trym. Her play *A Severed Head* was given its premiere at the Theatre Royal in King Street in 1963.

Peter Nichols, who was educated at Bristol Grammar School and trained at the Bristol Old Vic Theatre School, was a playwright and an actor. His plays included *A Day in the Death of Joe Egg*, *Privates on Parade* and *National Health*.

Christopher Fry, born in Bristol in 1907, became a teacher, actor and playwright who was regarded as one of the foremost dramatists of the mid-twentieth century. A phrase that Prime Minister Margaret Thatcher used in one of her speeches in 1980, 'The lady's not for turning', was a pun on Fry's play *The Lady's Not for Burning*.

The world premiere of Harold Pinter's first play *The Room* was performed by students from Bristol University's drama department in 1957. Pinter, who was aged 26 at the time, went on to become one of the country's most eminent dramatists. Forty-one years after the premiere the university awarded Pinter an honorary degree of Doctor of Letters.

BRISTOL PUBLISHERS

It's not generally known that the first edition of Jerome K. Jerome's novel *Three Men in a Boat* was brought out in 1889 by the family-owned publishing and book printing firm of J.W. Arrowsmith. Over the next few years the firm published two other books by Jerome. The firm also brought out *The Prisoner of Zenda* by Anthony Hope and the *Diary of a Nobody* by George and Weedon Grossmith. Arrowsmith's firm was based in a cellar in Quay Street on the edge of the City Docks.

Sir Allen Lane (1902–1970) who came from Cotham conceived the idea of cheap paperback books when he was looking for something to read while waiting for a train at Exeter railway station. At the time he was returning to London from a meeting with crime-thriller writer Agatha Christie. He came up with the idea of Penguin Books, now internationally known, and published his first one in 1935. It was a biography of the poet Shelley written by Andre Maurois and cost sixpence.

POET'S CORNER

Thomas Chatterton (1752–1770) is, arguably, Bristol's best-known poet. He is better known though for dying young – three months short of his eighteenth birthday – rather than his poetry. Chatterton, who was born opposite St Mary Redcliffe church, died of an overdose of drugs in a London garret in despair because his genius as a poet was unrecognised.

Studying old manuscripts that he found in Redcliffe church gave Chatterton the idea of inventing a medieval scholar and poet to whom he attributed his poems. For a while he was able to fool the public into believing them to be genuine. However, not getting the recognition he sought, Chatterton moved to London.

Not everyone who delivers the daily pint of milk has his or her portrait in the National Portrait Gallery, London. But Ann Yearsley (1756–1806), who delivered milk to her neighbours around Clifton Down, has not one but four portraits in the archive collection. Yearsley had a talent for writing poetry, historical plays and novels. Some of her poetry was shown to Hannah More who set about getting her verses published.

Sir Henry Newbolt (1862–1938), an 'old boy' of Clifton College, took up a career in law as a barrister but later turned to writing stories for boys, novels and a naval history as well as writing poetry. In all he wrote twenty-eight books and published twelve volumes of poetry. Some of his poetry was inspired by his days at Clifton College, especially the reference to the college's cricket pitch known as The Close:

> There's a breathless hush in the Close tonight –
> Ten to make and the match to win.

The appointment in 1863 of T.E. Brown as Second Master at Clifton College seemed to have inspired his poetry, too. He wrote several poems about the school and penned the immortal line 'A garden is a lovesome thing, God wot!' Brown is remembered at the college with one of the houses named after him.

Robert Southey, one of the founders of the Romantic Movement, was born above his father's linen shop in Wine Street in 1744. His name is included in the Baptismal Register of Christ Church, around the corner from his home. It was while he was living in Westbury-on-Trym that Southey wrote his *Eclogues*. He was Poet Laureate for thirty years until his death in 1843.

Joseph Cottle was a bookseller in Wine Street who paid Samuel Taylor Coleridge and Robert Southey thirty guineas each for their poems. He later gave Coleridge and William Wordsworth their big breakthrough by publishing their *Lyrical Ballads*.

Coleridge brought out the first edition in 1796 of his radical magazine *The Watchman* which was published from the historic Rummer Inn, in High Street. It carried the motto: 'That all may know the truth; and that the truth may make us free.' Coleridge's magazine included essays, parliamentary reports, book reviews, news stories and poems. The weekly publication had a short life, with readers being told in the tenth issue that 'the work did not pay the expenses'.

Isaac Rosenberg, the son of refugee Jewish parents, was born in the slums near Temple Meads station in 1890 and left school at the age of 14 but turned out to be a noted First World War poet. He wrote poems on scraps of paper in the trenches that he sent home to be typed. His *Poems from the Trenches* were published as a collection after the war. Rosenberg was killed in one of the Germans' last offensives in spring 1918. His name, along with those of fourteen other war poets, is carved on a stone in Poets' Corner at Westminster Abbey.

John Betjeman so loved the city that he even dedicated a poem to it. It begins:

> Green upon the flooded Avon shone the after-storm-wet-sky
> Quick the struggling withy branches let the leaves of autumn fly
> And a star shone over Bristol, wonderfully far and high

Anna Sewell, the author of *Black Beauty*, lived for six years in Blue Lodge, Abson, 11 miles north-east of Bristol. Some of the incidents in her book can be traced back to Sewell's time at Abson, including the time she saw a man killed by a passing cart.

READ ALL ABOUT IT!

Bristol's first newspaper – it was also one of the first provincial papers in the country – was the *Bristol Post-Boy*. Its first issue appeared in 1702 and was edited and printed by William Bonny. He arrived in the city from London and was given permission by the council to set up a printing press. The front page of his paper carried the strapline 'An account of the most material news, both foreign and domestic'. It is thought that the *Bristol Post-Boy* was published for about thirteen years.

Since the demise of the *Bristol Post-Boy* there have been many successors. Some lasted for just a few editions, like *The Postscript*, a Sunday newspaper that was published in June 1892 and survived for only three editions. Many of the newspapers were just one or two sheets of paper. They included:

1702 – *Bristol Post-Boy*
1715 – *Bristol Post Man*
1716 – *Bristol Weekly Mercury*
1742 – *The Oracle* (this was published by Andrew Hook while serving a prison sentence in Newgate Gaol for debt)
1748 – *The Weekly Intelligencer*
1752 – *Felix Farley's Bristol Journal*
1760 – *The Bristol Chronicle*
1767 – *The Bristol Gazette*
1774 – *The Bristol Journal*
1777 – *The Weekly Advertiser*
1817 – *Bristol Observer*
1827 – *The Bristolian*
1839 – *Bristol Times*
1850 – *Clifton Chronicle*
1853 – *Bristol Times and Bristol Journal*
1855 – *Bristol Advertiser*
1858 – *Western Daily Press*
1860 – *Bristol Daily Post*
1865 – *Daily Bristol Times and Mirror*
1877 – *Bristol Evening News*
1901 – *Bristol Echo*
1904 – *Bristol Evening Times*
1929 – *Bristol Evening World*
1932 – *Bristol Evening Post*

The West Country's first daily newspaper, the *Western Daily Press*, rolled off the presses in Bristol for the first time on 1 June 1858. The paper still has its editorial base in the city although it is no longer printed there. Since it was founded the paper has had several different owners but its name has never changed.

From the 1930s to the early 1960s Bristol had two evening newspapers, the *Evening Post* and the *Bristol Evening World*. However, the *World* folded in 1962 when its circulation was down to 30,000. Its title became incorporated with the *Post*.

On its first day in April 1932 the *Bristol Evening Post* sold 138,529 copies. There was a surplus of advertising that had to be held over until the next day. In the mid-1960s the paper was selling more than 160,000 copies a day. In August 2014 it was announced that the paper's circulation was down to 25,182.

THE FOURTH ESTATE

The origin of the phrase 'The Fourth Estate' in referring to the news media is often attributed to Edmund Burke MP for Bristol from 1774 to 1780. He apparently used it in a parliamentary debate on the opening of press reporting in the House of Commons.

10

TRANSPORTS OF DELIGHT

ON THE ROADS

In December 1705 the local council banned trucks from the city's roads unless they were made wholly of wood except for the banding of the wheels. A fine was imposed on offenders. This followed complaints that 'the great noise made by trucks by means of the iron materials about them is a great annoyance to inhabitants'.

A local newspaper reported in 1729: 'Following rain the road between Bristol and Bath became so flooded that several horsemen were forced to swim for their lives.' The passengers in the Bristol–Bath coach also had to swim out of the sunken coach.

The *Gentleman's Magazine* in 1754 reported that the Great West Road (the road from Bristol to London now known as the A4) was 'the worst possible public road in all Europe'.

A letter writer to a Bristol newspaper in 1792 claimed that there was so much mud on the Hotwells Road that carriage accidents were not to be feared as the ground was so soft 'consequently nothing but smothering remains to be dreaded'.

When the 1904 Motor Act came into force, industrialist Thomas Butler had the first registered car in Bristol. The number AE 1, which was allocated to his car, is now on the registration plate of the Lord Mayor of Bristol's official limousine.

A new road linking the centre of the city with Avonmouth and running underneath the Clifton Suspension Bridge was opened on 2 July 1926 by the Minister of Transport. The Portway had taken five years to build and cost £800,000, making it the most expensive highway to be built in the United Kingdom at the time. Work was delayed for twelve months when a section of a newly built embankment collapsed into the River Avon running alongside the road. The road, which is part of the national A4 route, is just over 5 miles long and for the most part 100ft wide.

The first spiral-ramp car park in the country was opened in Rupert Street in 1960. To mark the occasion hundreds of balloons were released, each carrying a ticket offering the finder free car parking for one day.

Bristol was the first city outside London to install parking meters. The cost of parking for two hours was 1s. Twenty-five men were recruited as parking wardens to make sure motorists did not overstay their welcome at a meter. A year later they were joined by a group of women whom the newspapers called 'meter maids'.

Motorists had a welcome Christmas present in 1971 when the M4 motorway linking Bristol and London was opened on 22 December. However, drivers leaving Bristol for London had to make sure they had enough fuel in their tanks as there was no service station for about 100 miles. It was another month before the Leigh Delamere service station in Wiltshire was opened.

Homes, shops, pubs and whole streets in Hotwells were demolished to make way for the £2,650 million Cumberland Basin Flyover, which was opened by the Minister of Transport in 1965. The scheme comprises a swing bridge over an entrance lock to the docks, a bridge over the River Avon and interchanges with several main roads. It was the first scheme of its kind to be built in Bristol to help traffic flow, especially when ships were entering or leaving the docks, by the use of carriageways at different levels. Within a couple of hours of being officially opened the Plimsoll Bridge section jammed open, causing a traffic jam.

ON THE RAILS

It seems that the Duke of Wellington was against the Great Western Railway. He is reported to have said: 'It will only encourage the lower classes to move about.'

The original Great Western Railway terminus at Temple Meads opened in 1840 with the first train leaving for Bath at 8 a.m. on 31 August 1840. The coaches were pulled by the steam locomotive *Fire Ball*.

A significant feature of the original terminus is the train shed, which for the first time for a railway station was roofed with a single span. It was constructed of timber, being 72ft (21.92m) wide and covering five broad-gauge rail tracks of 7ft (2.13m). Today the roof covers a car park for train passengers.

Besides the Great Western Railway, the Bristol and Exeter and Bristol and Gloucester railway companies shared the same terminus. In 1845 the Exeter Railway built its own station alongside that of the Great Western Railway.

The Bristolian express train ran from Bristol to London for the first time on 9 September 1935, marking the centenary of the Great Western Railway. It was the fastest train in Britain at the time, capable of reaching speeds in excess of 100mph. The engine used 7½ tons of coal on the journey between Temple Meads and Paddington. The Bristolian name has not been used since 1965.

The Bristol Harbour Railway, which opened in 1872, ran partly underground on its journey from Temple Meads railway station to the City Docks. Goods trains passed under St Mary Redcliffe churchyard to emerge beside the Ostrich pub at Bathurst Basin and then on to the dockside. The tunnel has long been sealed.

The driver and fireman of the *Flying Dutchman* express were killed when their train left the track and overturned at Long Ashton on 28 July 1876. Fifteen passengers and the two guards had to be treated for their injuries. The accident happened just a few miles short of the train's next stop at Temple Meads station. An accident inquiry found that the train, carrying 200 passengers, was travelling at 60mph. The cause of the crash was identified as poor track maintenance.

When British Rail launched its new 125mph High Speed Train service in 1976 it chose the London (Paddington) to Bristol route for the first train. Passengers paid £5 for a return ticket. The first train arrived at Temple Meads station three minutes early.

Train operator *First Great Western* put its longest-ever commemorative nameplate on a power car to mark the bi-centenary of Isambard Kingdom Brunel's birth in 2006. The nameplate measured 1.65m long and featured a head and shoulders silhouette of Brunel wearing his trademark stovepipe top hat.

ON THE BUSES

When it was announced that the first horse-drawn trams in Bristol would run into Clifton there was much protest by people living there. Letter writers to the local papers protested that 'hordes of working-class people' would arrive in the leafy suburb. Churchgoers believed that the trams would encourage 'workers to seek out sinful pleasures'. One letter writer from Clifton to the *Bristol Mercury* asked: 'Is it not something terrible that the disgusting tramway is to bring the nasty low inhabitants of Bristol up to our sacred region?'

Undeterred, Bristol Tramways, a private company, launched the service in August 1875. The first horse-drawn tram, with a top speed of 6mph, left Perry Road near Bristol Royal Infirmary on a route which took it past the Victoria Rooms and up Whiteladies Road to St John's church on the corner of Apsley Road, a journey of just over a mile and a half. The service was so popular that in the first month more than 100,000 passengers had made the journey. Horse-drawn trams were later extended to other parts of the city.

By 1881 eighty-five trams were in use and 300 horses employed to pull them. Men were specially taken on by the tramway company to clear the streets of horse manure and deliver it to market gardens on the edge of the city.

Bristol's first motor bus ran from Clifton Suspension Bridge to the Victoria Rooms on 17 January 1906. It had seats for nineteen passengers on the top deck, sixteen inside and two more beside the driver. The service ran every ten minutes and the fare was one penny. The service was eventually extended across the city.

In 1912 the Bristol Tramways Company bought a funicular railway that ran through a specially excavated tunnel in the rocks of the Avon Gorge. Its carriages carried passengers from Hotwells to Sion Hill close to Clifton Suspension Bridge. However, it was closed down in 1934 with the owners saying it was no longer economical. The Rocks Railway originally opened in March 1893 with more than 6,200 passengers using it on the first day. The journey took just forty seconds.

When the Royal Show was held in 1913 on Clifton and Durdham Downs, 225 trams were diverted from their normal routes to take 1.5 million visitors to the showground.

Staff at shops, offices and factories were given time off to watch the first electric tram in the city go into service. It ran from Old Market to Kingswood and was so successful that electric trams were gradually introduced across the city.

The tramway company's 237 trams were all open-topped and made up what was believed to be the largest fleet of open-topped trams in the British Isles.

The electric tram service ran until April 1941 when it was brought to an abrupt end by a bomb that fell near the power station, cutting the electricity supply.

Bristol's first coach station was officially called the Bristol Travel Bureau and Cafe. It opened in Prince Street in 1930 and was in operation until 1954 when a more modern bus station was built at Marlborough Street.

West Indian activists boycotted the city's buses for four months in 1963. It was a protest against Bristol Omnibus Company's refusal to employ black or Asian crews on its buses. The company's ban was discussed in Parliament, the national press and protest marches were staged in Bristol. The boycott was lifted when the company dropped its colour ban. Campaigners claim that their boycott led to the UK's first-ever laws against racial-based discrimination.

UP IN THE AIR

When he officially opened Bristol Airport on 31 March 1930, the Duke of Kent's speech was broadcast nationally. This was only the third civil airport in the country. It was created through a group of businessmen who had spent £16,386 on land at Whitchurch, 3 miles south of the city centre, to be developed by the Bristol and Wessex Aeroplane Club as an airport. In its first year 935 passengers used the airport. Bristol's southern boundary was extended to take in the airport.

The first international flight by Aer Lingus on 27 May 1936 from Dublin to Whitchurch Airport was made amidst a blaze of publicity but turned out to be embarrassing for all concerned. The plane, after being blessed by the Irish Air Corps chaplain, took off at 9 a.m. and was due to land at Whitchurch two hours later. However, the de Havilland Dragon Rapide touched down fifty-five minutes late because of a problem with its radio.

Whitchurch Airport was requisitioned by the Air Ministry between 1940–45. All Imperial Airways and BA flights were transferred to the airport, which was the only airport in the UK where civilian aircraft were allowed to take off and land.

As passenger numbers grew, Whitchurch Airport was replaced by a new development at Lulsgate Bottom, 7 miles south-west of Bristol, in 1957. Bristol City Council paid £55,000 for the site, a disused RAF airfield, which became known as Bristol (Lulsgate) Airport. The council ran the airport until 1997 when a majority shareholding was sold to a private transport operator.

The airport's name was changed in 1997 to Bristol International Airport. It changed again in 2010 to its present name, Bristol Airport.

This is now the UK's fifth largest airport outside London with 6.1 million passengers using it in 2013. The airport experienced the busiest day in its history on 14 August 2014 when a total of 25,390 passengers passed through the terminal in twenty-four hours.

The airport now has flights to more than 100 destinations. It is also a major employer in Bristol and north Somerset with 3,000 staff working on the site.

A plaque at the airport commemorates the life of Hollywood actor Leslie Howard and sixteen other people who were killed when their plane was attacked by eight German Junkers JU 88 aircraft on 1 June 1943. It happened when their DC3 aircraft was flying over the Bay of Biscay from Portugal to Bristol during the Second World War and crashed into the sea.

Crowds gathered around Clifton Suspension Bridge in November 1910 to witness the first-ever aircraft fly over it. At the controls was a French pilot, Maurice Tetard, who was giving a public demonstration of the Bristol Boxkite aircraft built by the British and Colonial Aeroplane Company at Filton. The Boxkite both took off and landed on Durdham Downs near the Sea Walls.

BRIDGING THE GAP

For a relatively small city in size, Bristol probably has more bridges than many a larger town. There are nearly fifty bascular bridges, footbridges and swivel bridges, mainly crossing two waterways, the River Avon and the Floating Harbour.

The best-known bridge is, of course, Isambard Kingdom Brunel's Clifton Suspension Bridge. It was built after wine merchant William Vick, who died in 1754, left £1,000 to be invested together with its accumulated interest until it reached £10,000. Vick wanted to build a stone bridge spanning the River Avon at Clifton. In the event the bridge cost more than £100,000.

In his will Vick stipulated that the bridge should be toll free forever, but this condition was dropped many years ago.

When Brunel submitted his designs for the bridge he was in Bristol recovering from injuries he received while working for his father in the Rotherhithe Tunnel under the River Thames.

Brunel submitted not one design but four. One of them included then fashionable Egyptian sphinxes on top of each of the bridge's piers. They were dropped, presumably, because of the cost.

Work on the bridge started in 1831 but was dogged by financial problems and it was not finished until 1864. Brunel described it as 'my first child, my darling'. Unfortunately he died five years before it was opened. The bridge was completed as a monument to him.

Many tens of thousands of people lined the streets and hillsides around the bridge for its official opening on 8 December 1864. Besides organised firework displays, people in the crowd let off their own sparklers and squibs. One man reported 'ruthless burning of the whiskers on one side only'.

To make sure she was the first person to cross the bridge, Mary Griffiths, aged 21 from Hanham, ran across it hoping that no one would overtake her.

The Latin motto on the Clifton Pier of the bridge reads *Suspensa vix via fit*. It is loosely translated as 'a suspended way made with difficulty'.

The road itself is 3ft higher on the Clifton side than the Leigh Woods end. Brunel deliberately designed the bridge this way to create a level appearance because of the topography of the area.

On its opening day, 8 December 1864, the bridge was lit up for two hours. Other major occasions when it was illuminated include:

The Bristol-France Week in 1931 when the bridge was lit by 1,500 electric lights.

King George's Jubilee in 1935, which was celebrated with 3,000 lights switched on for a month.

The Festival of Britain in 1951, which saw 4,500 lamps lit up every night during the summer.

The coronation of Queen Elizabeth II in 1953, which was marked with more than 5,600 lamps being switched on from June until the end of August.

During the Queen's Silver Jubilee the bridge was illuminated throughout the summer.

Since the 200th anniversary of Brunel's birth in 2006, the lights on the bridge have been on every day. The bridge trustees say that the cost of electricity used is no more than what the occupier of a detached house would pay for having all the appliances on.

Every year around 3 million cars and vans cross the bridge, which was built in the days of the horse and cart.

UNUSUAL EVENTS ON OR AROUND CLIFTON SUSPENSION BRIDGE

In 1957 Pilot Officer John Crossley flew a de Havilland Vampire jet, capable of flying at up to 400mph, under the bridge. Unfortunately the plane crashed into the Leigh Woods side of the Avon Gorge, killing the pilot. No one has flown under the bridge since.

Footballer and *Match of the Day* presenter Gary Lineker was filmed driving a tractor across the bridge in 2013 as part of a television commercial for a certain brand of potato crisps.

OTHER BRISTOL BRIDGES BY BRUNEL

While he was working in Clifton, Brunel also built two other bridges in Bristol. The Avon Bridge, built in 1839, still carries trains across the River Avon at Brislington into Temple Meads railway station. It is designated by English Heritage as a Grade I listed structure. Ten years later Brunel built his first tubular swing, or swivel bridge. It originally carried traffic over an entrance lock of the Cumberland Basin but was made redundant when the Cumberland Basin Flyover was opened in 1965. For more than half a century the bridge has been lying virtually abandoned on the dockside beneath the flyover where it has been left to rust and rot.

MORE INTERESTING BRIDGES AND THE FERRIES THEY REPLACED

Ashton Swing Bridge was built in 1906 as a two-level road and railway bridge as part of the Bristol Harbour Railway. During the planning stages it was agreed that the estimated cost of £36,500 would be shared by Bristol City Council and the Great Western Railway (GWR). In the event it cost £70,389 but GWR only paid an extra £4,000. The bridge was last swung in 1934 and the road deck removed in 1965. It now forms part of a local access cycle and footpath. The bridge is listed by English Heritage as a Grade I structure.

Prince Street Bridge in the City Docks was opened in 1809 and replaced an ancient ferry in the Floating Harbour that was run by the Dean and Chapter of Bristol Cathedral.

St Philip's Bridge, built in 1841, was known as Halfpenny Bridge because of the price of the original toll. The tolls were dropped in 1875.

Vauxhall Bridge, built in 1900, which crosses the River Avon or New Cut, and links the suburbs of Southville and Ashton with Hotwells, was originally a swing bridge. However, it hasn't been swung since 1935 and ever since has been a footbridge.

Gaol Ferry Bridge, which links Southville with the city centre, replaces a ferry service that crossed the River Avon for more than 100 years. In its first twenty-five years the ferry carried more than 1 million passengers who were charged a penny for each crossing. The bridge was built in 1935 at a cost of £2,000 near the old gaol and the slipway to the ferry, which is still there.

The M5 Avonmouth Bridge is a road bridge of eight lanes that carries traffic on the motorway over the River Avon from Bristol into Somerset and, of course, the other way. The bridge cost £4,200,000 and when it was opened in May 1974 it brought an end to the Pill Ferry which for many decades carried commuters from the north Somerset village of Pill to Shirehampton on the Bristol side of the River Avon. Initially they made the crossing in a rowing boat but this was replaced by a motorboat in 1935.

Aust Ferry, which crossed the River Severn between Aust and Beachley for many years, made its last journey on 8 September 1966 when Queen Elizabeth II opened the Severn Bridge. There had been talk for more than 150 years of building a road across the Severn about 10 miles upstream from Bristol. But it wasn't until 1961 that construction work actually started.

The Severn Bridge has a main span of 3,240ft and the entire structure cost £8 million. More than 300 million vehicles have crossed the bridge since it opened.

The original Severn Bridge toll for cars was 2*s* 6*d* (12p). At the time, Geoffrey Milner of the AA was reported in newspapers as saying: 'By the year 2000 the question of tolls should not arise. By that time the capital cost of the £8 million bridge should have been paid. Once that happens the tolls will be removed.'

Welcoming the opening of the Severn Bridge the Lord Mayor of Bristol, Councillor Cyril Hebblethwaite, said: 'To our friends in South Wales I say, "Come and see us often". To my fellow citizens of Bristol I say, "Go over to Wales, enjoy the many attractions the Welsh have to offer and meet as many of the people of Wales as you can".'

Thirty years after his mother opened the first Severn Bridge, Prince Charles opened the Second Severn Crossing, which was designed to alleviate traffic on the original bridge. This is a six-lane motorway, which is part of the M4 motorway and took four years to build. The crossing stands at the lowest limit of the River Severn and the start of the Severn Estuary.

Pero's Bridge, spanning St Augustine's Reach in the City Docks, is named after the slave of a wealthy merchant, John Pinney. It was built in 1999 and commemorates all those who were enslaved by Bristol merchants. It is a pedestrian bascule bridge with decks that rise to allow ships in and out of the Reach.

11

ON THE AIRWAVES

AUNTIE COMES TO BRISTOL

The BBC began broadcasting in Bristol in 1931 with a team of three people working in a studio that had been installed above a bank in The Triangle, Clifton.

Larger premises for what was to become the BBC's West Region headquarters were found the following year in a most unusual way. Two executives from London searching for suitable premises spotted an empty villa on the corner of Whiteladies Road and Tyndalls Park Road for sale. As there was no estate agent on hand with the keys the executives made their way into the building by climbing through a coal cellar window. They liked what they saw inside and the villa became – and still is – part of the BBC campus.

Broadcasting House, Bristol, was officially opened by the Lord Mayor on 18 September 1934. Originally there were four studios, each one designated for a particular use. Two were for talks and drama, a third for sound effects and the fourth was big enough to hold a full orchestra. One of the early broadcasters was John Betjeman who had been booked to give talks about architecture. He later became much better known as a poet.

At the outbreak of the Second World War the BBC moved its Variety Department out of London to Bristol, believing the West Country would be relatively safer from bombing. Various light entertainment programmes like *It's That Man Again* with Tommy Handley were broadcast from parish halls around Bristol, designed to keep morale up. BBC staff called it the Fun Factory.

The BBC's Symphony Orchestra conducted by Sir Adrian Boult performed in a railway tunnel in the Avon Gorge for one performance only – but nobody heard the music. Sir Adrian was checking the acoustics in case the orchestra had to play in the tunnel during the war. He was happy with the result and reported back to the BBC's Director General. However, before any arrangements could be made for the musicians to move in, the tunnel on the disused Bristol Port and Railway line had been taken over by local people as an air-raid shelter.

A long-running soap opera called *At The Luscombes* was launched by the BBC in Bristol in September 1948. Each weekly episode ran for twenty minutes and featured the life of the Luscombe family and the fictional village of Dimstock set between Salisbury and Warminster in the Wylye Valley. Although the series could only be heard on the BBC's West Region service it was a forerunner of another radio soap opera, *The Archers*, which started in 1951.

Poetry Please is the longest-running poetry programme in the world. It started in 1979 and is still produced in Bristol for transmission on Radio 4.

The *Antiques Roadshow*, first broadcast from Bristol in 1979, still attracts an audience of between 6 and 8 million viewers each week. It is a successor to a previous antiques programme called *Going for a Song*, which made a household name of antiques dealer Arthur Negus. Up to the end of 2014 *Antiques Roadshow* had visited 534 venues. Viewers have taken about 9 million objects to the shows to be valued.

BBC Television launched its West Region news service from Bristol in September 1957. Initially, its nightly news magazine *News West* – a forerunner of *Points West* – was five minutes long but was later extended to the present half an hour. The news-reading team was led by senior announcer Hugh Shiriff, who always appeared on screen wearing his trademark buttonhole carnation.

Actress Armine Sandford was the first woman to read the news on BBC regional television when she presented the West Region's daily news bulletins from the Bristol studios in 1957.

Britain's first reality television show went on the air in 1977. Six couples and three young children aged 2, 4, and 6 years, were taken back twenty-three centuries in a bid to recapture how people survived around 300 BC. For a year the fifteen people lived in an Iron Age settlement that had been reconstructed by BBC producers in Bristol at a secret location on the Somerset-Wiltshire border. The volunteers dressed, ate, worked and slept Iron Age style for a series called *Living in the Past*. The volunteers, who included a doctor, a jobbing builder and teachers, were given a fee of £20 a week.

Although the BBC's Natural History Unit, based in Bristol, was not founded as such until 1957, a radio programme called *The Naturalist* was first broadcast on 3 January 1946. The Natural History Unit makes more than 25 per cent of the world's natural history films.

Sir David Attenborough's *Life On Earth* series launched in 1979 cost more than £1 million to make. More than 500 million viewers worldwide watched the programmes, which took three years to make.

To make the programmes, which the BBC described as its 'first television mega-series', twenty cameramen travelled a total of 1.5 million miles around the globe.

The *Animal Magic* programme, affectionately called Animal Tragic by BBC staff, went on the air for the first time in 1962 and ran for twenty-one years. It was presented each week by Johnny Morris in his role as a zookeeper and was the first big television hit show featuring animals. Sometimes programmes were filmed in the studios and other times at Bristol Zoo. Johnny Morris provided voices for animals, appearing to make them talk. Morris, who had been a farm manager, was 'discovered' by a BBC producer who heard him telling anecdotes in his local pub.

One of the most unusual requests dealt with by the producers of *Points West* came from film actress Sophia Loren. She asked for a bed to be installed in the boardroom so that she could rest before being interviewed on the regional television news.

TWENTY FORMER AND PRESENT BBC WEST PRESENTERS/REPORTERS

John Norman
Peter Brown (industrial reporter)
Tom Salmon
Jeremy Carrad (presenter)
Mike Dornan
Amanda Thuenissen
Nicholas Tresillian
Sue Carpenter
Sally Challoner
Susan Osman (presenter)
Chris Vacher (presenter)
Sheila Young
Amanda Parr
Mark Puckle
Malcolm Frith (business reporter)
Jemma Cooper (weather reporter)
Alex Lovell (presenter)
Richard Angwin (weather presenter)
David Dimbleby
Jonathan Dimbleby

Chris Vacher notched up the record for being the longest-serving main anchorman of *Points West*. He sat in front of the camera for twenty-eight years, making his final appearance on 9 December 2011. Before joining the BBC Chris Vacher spent the 1970s with the Royal Navy. He served for a time on a frigate and learnt basic Russian.

Jeremy Carrad was the main frontman of *Points West* for fourteen years in the 1960s/'70s.

David Dimbleby and his younger brother Jonathan both started their BBC careers in Bristol. David was a news reporter in the 1960s and Jonathan worked for *Points West* about the same time.

ITV ARRIVES IN THE WEST

Independent Television arrived in West Country homes when Television Wales and West (TWW) went on the air for the first time in 1958. Announcer Bruce Lewis told the viewers: 'We are brimful of happiness to be on the air.'

TWW had built its own studio at Arnos Vale from which to operate the ten-year franchise it had been given by the Independent Television Authority.

The station's launch night line-up included a variety programme starring Harry Secombe, Shirley Bassey, Tommy Cooper and Sir Ralph Richardson. TWW devised its own quiz show *The £1,000 Word*, which was broadcast for the first time that night. Bert Tann, manager of Bristol Rovers Football Club, was one of the winning contestants.

TWW's franchise was not renewed by the Independent Television Authority. No reason was publicly given for this but it was reported that the ITA was not happy that the broadcaster had its headquarters in London, which was seen to be too far removed from its West Country viewers. When the station closed down in March 1968 the last voice to be heard on air was that of the poet John Betjeman with a eulogy that ironically was recorded in a London studio and not in Bristol.

Harlech Television, a consortium of mainly West Country business-men, backed by well-known names including actors Richard Burton and Stanley Baker, and broadcaster Wynford Vaughan Thomas, succeeded TWW and moved into their old studios. The consortium was led by Lord Harlech, who until 1964, when he inherited his father's title, was David Ormsby-Gore. He was a politician who was once Britain's ambassador in America.

The new television company announced its arrival in Bristol with all the show-business razzmatazz it could muster. Richard Burton and Liz Taylor were among the celebrities that turned up at the official launch party at the studios in 1968. The newspapers paid more attention to the news that Taylor and Burton had just announced their engagement rather than Harlech's programme schedules. Photographers' cameras were focused on Miss Taylor's engagement ring, which had been reportedly bought for £127,000.

The events that happened on Harlech's first night were certainly not on the script. It was supposed to broadcast a recorded message from the Head of the Independent Television Authority but instead viewers were treated to footage of Harry Secombe in drag being chased around a four-poster bed by Bruce Forsyth in a bedroom romp. The reason for the 'technical hitch' was never explained to the viewers.

Two years after being on air, Harlech changed its station identity to HTV to avoid any suggestions of Welsh bias although the company had studios in Cardiff broadcasting to Wales.

Besides regional programming, HTV gained a reputation for its full-length feature films, including *The Master of Ballantrae*, *The Canterville Ghost*, which starred John Gielgud, and *Jamaica Inn*. Actors like John Geilgud, Lawrence Olivier, Brian Blessed and Oliver Tobias were contracted to appear in HTV dramas.

In 2004 HTV lost its on-screen regional identity with all the regional independent television franchises in the country going under the control of ITV plc.

TWENTY FORMER AND PRESENT HTV WEST PRESENTERS/REPORTERS

Bruce Hockin (presenter)
Gillian Miles
Annie Mckie
Richard Wyatt (presenter)
Patsy Yorston
Sherrie Eugene
Alison Holloway
Marjorie Lofthouse
Polly Lloyd (also worked for BBC Radio Bristol)
John Abrams (gardening expert)

Gill Impey (weather reporter)
Bob Crampton
Graham Purches (at one time he was a BBC West presenter)
Rebecca Pow
Bob Constantine
Elise Rayner
Julia Caesar
Graham Miller (sports presenter)
Liza Aziz
Jane Solomons

Bruce Hockin became ITV's longest-serving regional news presenter when he retired from HTV in 1996. He began his television career with TWW in the 1960s, joined HTV and worked in television for more than three decades.

TELEVISION WEDDING

Alison Holloway met her former husband, comedian Jim Davidson, while interviewing him for HTV West news programmes about his role in a pantomime at Bristol Hippodrome. Thousands of people packed the streets around the register office in Quaker's Friars where the couple married in 1987. They were divorced two years later.

TV PROGRAMMES MADE IN BRISTOL

Casualty, a primetime Saturday night emergency drama television series, was made in the city for more than twenty years. A former warehouse in St Philips was turned into the fictional Holby City hospital while many landmarks across Bristol were used as locations for outdoor scenes. Despite a campaign by actors and viewers to keep *Casualty* in the city the BBC transferred it in 2011 to its Cardiff studios.

Parts of *Only Fools and Horses*, a sitcom starring David Jason as market trader Derek 'Del' Boy Trotter and his younger brother Rodney, were shot in Bristol although the series was set in Peckham, south London. A tower block of flats at Ashton Gate became Peckham's Mandela House while a nearby car firm was used as a showroom where the Trotter brothers looked at a Rolls-Royce. Scenes where Del and Rodney ran down a street dressed as Batman and Robin were filmed in Broadmead.

Being Human was a supernatural drama-comedy series broadcast on BBC 3 in 2008. It starred Leonara Crichlow, Russell Tovey and Aidan Turner as three people sharing a home in Bristol and trying to live a normal life despite being a ghost, a werewolf and a vampire respectively.

Bristol's answer to *Sex and the City* was a series called *Mistresses*, which was filmed at various locations across the city. The series followed four women through the trials and tribulations of their lives.

One of the first comprehensive schools to open in Bristol in the 1960s took on the role of the fictional Summerdown School in the Channel 4 series *Teachers*.

LOCAL RADIO

BBC Radio Bristol went on air for the first time on 4 September 1970 broadcasting from a house in Tyndalls Park Road that had been converted into a radio station with three studios. The arrival of local radio meant that the West Region radio programmes disappeared. These included *Today in the South West* which was an opt out from the national *Today* programme every morning and broadcast from the Clifton studios.

Radio Bristol's early broadcasting staff included Kate Adie who went on to become the BBC's Chief News Correspondent reporting from war zones around the world. One of her first reporting assignments for Radio Bristol was the annual Bristol Flower Show on Clifton Downs.

Journalist Michael Buerke, who later became better known as a television newsreader, and Jenni Murray, who presents Radio 4's *Woman's Hour* which she joined in 1987, were also with Radio Bristol in its early days. Jenni Murray was made a Dame in the Queen's Birthday Honours of 2011.

Former *Bristol Evening Post* Chief Reporter Roger Bennett joined the station from its inception becoming the longest-serving breakfast show presenter on radio. He fronted the *Morning West* programme for more than twenty-eight years. Roger was also well known for leading the Blue Notes Jazz Band on soprano sax and clarinet since the group started in 1956 until his untimely death in 2005.

Another *Evening Post* chief reporter, Nigel Dando, has been with Radio Bristol since 2001.

BANNED BY THE BBC

Four-piece rock group *The Cougars* saw their record 'Saturday Nite at the Duck Pond' reach number thirty-three – its highest point – in the UK single records chart in 1963. Although it stayed in the chart for two months the BBC banned the Bristol group's record from being played on air. The Corporation said it was unsuitable as the music was a 'hotted up' version of Tchaikovsky's *Swan Lake* ballet.

'Drink up thy Zider', which was recorded by Bristol's 'Scrumpy and Western' band the Wurzels, entered the pop charts at the number forty-five slot in 1966. The BBC, however, banned their disc jockeys from playing the record's 'B' side *Twice Daily*. The Corporation claimed it was 'too raunchy'.

INDEPENDENT RADIO

Radio West was the first commercial radio station in Bristol which had its studios on the city's dockside. The station went on air for the first time on 27 October 1981. The first voice that listeners heard was that of Dave Cash, a Capital Radio, London, presenter, who had been appointed Radio West's programme controller.

The company backing Radio West issued 600,000 non-voting £1 shares and £400,000 unsecured loan stock. But the station faced financial problems as well as low audience figures. It broadcast as Radio West for the last time on 8 September 1985. The station then merged with Wilshire Radio, which was relaunched as GWR.

Bristol Hospital Broadcasting service puts out its programmes from a studio in Bristol Royal Infirmary. The station made its first broadcast in August 1952 with a match report from the Bristol Rovers–Shrewsbury game at Eastville Stadium. The station can be heard by patients in eight hospitals across the city and is one of the oldest surviving hospital broadcasters in the country.

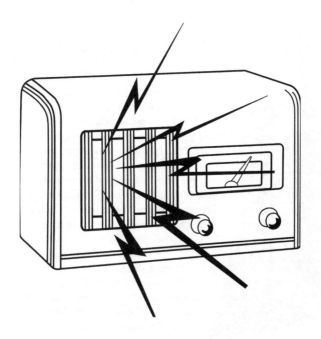

12

LAW AND ORDER

THE 'BLOODY ASSIZE'

Judge Jeffreys came to Bristol to hold part of his bloody assize after the Monmouth Rebellion of 1685. He spent two days in the city holding his court on the site of the present Guildhall. A Grand Jury of forty-one men were empanelled and Judge Jeffreys eventually condemned six men to hang, although three were later reprieved. The executions took place on Redcliffe Hill.

LEGAL EAGLES COME TO TOWN

Judges who arrived in Bristol from London in the eighteenth century to hear cases at the courts were entertained in rather grand style by the city fathers. One judge, Mr Justice Powell, was given six gallons of sherry and twelve quarts of claret. The city council may not be as generous in these times of austerity but it still provides accommodation, known as the Judges' Lodgings in Clifton for High Court judges who hear cases at the Crown Court. The High Sheriff of Bristol is now expected to entertain the judges at his or her own cost.

High Court judges, barristers and solicitors, all bewigged and robed, maintain an historic tradition when they make their way in procession from the City Hall to Bristol Cathedral every October for the

Legal Sunday service. This marks the start of the legal year and the Michaelmas Law Term. The lawyers are joined by the Lord Mayor and city councillors, also in their robes. Until the assize courts were abolished in 1971 and replaced by the Crown Court, judges arrived at court in a horse-drawn carriage.

Solicitors in the city founded the first law society in the country in 1770. It means that Bristol Law Society is senior to the Law Society of England and Wales by fifty-five years. One of the Bristol society's early rules was that meetings should start at 'seven o'clock in the evening and continue until half an hour after ten, when the Tavern Bill shall be called for and discharged'.

The oldest surviving legal practice in England, Latchams, Montague, Niblett, opened their doors for business in 1710 at Stokes Croft. Some years ago the practice merged with another Bristol law firm.

One of the most unusual scenes to occur at the Old Bailey happened when John Noble the Mayor of Bristol in 1792 exercised an ancient privilege granted to his city.

Dressed in his robes he claimed a seat next to a judge who was trying prisoners. The astonished judge demanded an explanation. Mr Noble told him that by an ancient charter successive Mayors of Bristol were constituted judges of the court. After asserting his right the mayor saluted the judge and left the court.

LAST MAN TO BE HANGED ON THE DOWNS

The *Bristol Journal* reported in 1819 that 'roads leading to Clifton are so infested at night with desperadoes that few gentlemen think it safe to walk about alone or unarmed'.

Shenkin Protheroe had the rather dubious distinction of being the last person to be hung on a gibbet at Gallows Acre Lane, the highest point of Clifton and Durdham Downs, in 1873. At that time the Downs was a dangerous and desolate place frequented by the likes of highwaymen and footpads. One of them was Protheroe, who ingratiated himself with passing travellers before attacking and robbing them. On one occasion his victim, a pig drover, died and Protheroe was hung. The bodies of murderers were often left in a cage swinging from the gibbet in the wind.

DOWNS LAWS

A by-law was introduced on Clifton and Durdham Downs in 1892 that banned carpet beating after complaints that it was a nuisance. People living in large houses on the edge of the Downs had been beating their carpets for some years on specially erected wooden posts. The situation got worse when carpet-beating companies joined them.

Other by-laws prohibit the erection of tents, hanging up of any linen for drying or bleaching, throwing of stones or sticks, flower picking and rock collecting. The law also bans fighting and swearing, the telling of fortunes or selling infamous books or prints as well as using windsurfing and speed sailing machines.

HOW TO APPEAR BEFORE THE COURTS

At the spring quarter sessions in 1712 John Boroston was charged with pretending to be a Clerk in Holy Orders and defrauding people of their money by 'clandestinely marrying them'. He charged each couple he married 18*d*.

In medieval days bakers who sold underweight bread were put in a cage in Wine Street so that the public could easily spot the wrong-doers.

Fishmongers who sold bad fish were forced to walk through the city wearing collars of rotting fish.

A butcher was convicted on 17 June 1736 of exposing for sale in Broad Street an old ewe 'dressed up in the same manner as a lamb'. He was fined £2.

Two barbers were placed in the stocks in Temple Street for having shaved customers on a Sunday in 1775.

A soldier convicted of stealing a shirt was sentenced by court martial to receive 1,000 lashes, reported *The Bristol Journal* in 1775. On hearing of his sentence the soldier nearly killed himself by cutting his throat. The court then reduced his punishment to 200 lashes. The soldier was also drummed out of his regiment.

John Edgar, a member of the Common Council, appeared before the court in September 1805 accused of refusing to become Mayor of Bristol for the coming year. He was fined £400.

Francis Greenway is remembered as the 'father' of Sydney's classical architecture although he had been transported from Bristol for fraud. He was said to have forged a promissory note for £250 while involved with a building contract in Clifton. Greenway, who designed the Assembly Rooms – now the Clifton Club – in The Mall was sentenced to death. However, in 1811 he won a reprieve and was transported. He designed many of Sydney's public buildings and his portrait was put on some of Australia' ten dollar bills.

In 1815 the Earl of Pembroke, the Lord Lieutenant of Bristol, was fined and committed to the Tower for taking precedence of the Mayor of Bristol.

Every parish had its own set of wooden stocks, usually in the parish churchyard. The last recorded use of the stocks was in 1828. Three men were arrested for 'carousing' in St Mary Redcliffe churchyard shortly before a funeral was due to take place. They refused to pay their fines and the magistrates ordered them to be 'exposed for three hours' in the stocks on Redcliffe Hill. The punishment was ordered to be carried out immediately.

Thirteen-year-old Frederick Parker appeared before Bristol magistrates in August 1907 where he admitted stealing two razors from his former employers. Although he produced good references to the court from his headmaster and Sunday school superintendent, the court ordered that Parker should receive eight strokes of the birch in front of his father.

William Finney, who styled himself as a professor, planned to dive head first from Clifton Suspension Bridge into the River Avon in 1902. However, the police, having been tipped off, reached the scene before Finney could make his attempt. He was arrested and appeared in court later the same day when he was accused of 'being about the bridge and being there for an unlawful purpose'. Finney was bound over to be of good behaviour for six months.

Fred Little, the owner of a postcard shop in Old Market Street, was charged at the magistrates' court in September 1913 with exposing and offering for sale obscene and indecent postcards. The court heard that a police officer had seized 20,000 cards. Little argued that they were not obscene but the magistrates rejected his defence. They ordered that the cards should be destroyed and fined Little £5.

The royal charter granted to Bristol in 1373 gave the new county various privileges, including the right to have a town jail. This was built at Newgate, and known by that name, on a site now occupied by the car park of the Galleries shopping centre. Prison inmates had to rely on the generosity of the local people for food as no meals were then provided by the prison authorities.

THE BOYS IN BLUE

Bristol was one of the first cities in the country to form a professional police force. The local constabulary was founded on 25 June 1836. Joseph Bishop of the Metropolitan Police Force, which had been formed seven years earlier, was appointed Superintendent of Police. He had 227 men – made up of one superintendent, four inspectors, twenty-four sergeants, 197 constables and one clerk – under his command.

Each policeman was issued with a top hat, blue coat and white trousers. At night officers went on duty equipped with a rattle, lamp and a staff.

It seems that a policeman's lot was not always a happy one for in the first six weeks of the formation of the constabulary thirteen officers quit and a further thirteen were dismissed.

The first chief constable for the Bristol police force was appointed in 1884.

Britain's first training school for female police officers was set up by the Bristol force during the First World War. The school's director, Dorothy Peto, was later appointed the first head of the Metropolitan Police Women's Division.

The Avon and Somerset Constabulary was formed in 1974 from the merger of the old Somerset and Bath Constabulary with Bristol and the Staple Hill division of the Gloucestershire force. The force serves a population of nearly 1.5 million people across 1,855 square miles taking in towns, cities, seaside resorts, farms, moorland and forests. About 6,700 are employed by the force from frontline officers to support staff.

Avon and Somerset Constabulary moved from its headquarters in Bridewell, in the centre of the city in 1995, into purpose-built offices at Portishead. They were built on a 47-acre site which cost £31 million. The new headquarters was officially opened by the queen, who was presented with a truncheon made of Bristol Blue glass.

The first case in the world of using DNA to convict a rapist was at Bristol Crown Court in 1987. After hearing the DNA results the defendant pleaded guilty and was sentenced to eight years' imprisonment.

Councillor Tom Turvey, chairman of the local police authority, pulled no punches when in 1985 he described St George police station as the 'worst in the British Isles'. His catalogue of failures included poor lighting, unheated cells and poor drainage. Work started on improving the station but in 1997 it was closed. The building, which was built in 1881, has since been turned into residential accommodation.

The police station built in the 1950s as headquarters for officers patrolling the City Docks is now a restaurant, called River Station. It still has the slipway into the harbour for the patrol boat. The river police, part of Avon and Somerset Constabulary, were disbanded after the docks were closed to commercial shipping.

IN MEMORY OF A POLICEMAN

A plaque in Trinity Road police station commemorates the life of Police Constable Richard Hill, aged 31, who was murdered while off-duty and wearing plain clothes. He was stabbed to death in the groin while trying to intervene in an argument over the ill-treatment of a donkey in 1869. The incident happened in a street off Old Market Street and carried over into a pub where PC Hill was stabbed. Thousands of citizens lined the streets for PC Hill's funeral at Arnos Vale cemetery.

SOME MAJOR CRIMINAL INCIDENTS

A total of twelve people were killed and forty-five injured when riots flared in 1793 in protest over the renewal of tolls on Bristol Bridge.

Hundreds of people were involved in the riots of 1831, which started after the House of Lords rejected the Second Reform Bill. The riots lasted three days, during which people were killed or injured and public and private buildings set alight and looted. Much of the rioting was centred around Queen Square. Four of the ringleaders were hanged while many others were transported.

Several hundred rioters broke away from the main mob and pulled down the gates of the prison on nearby Cumberland Road. They were armed with hatchets, crowbars and sledgehammers. A small boy who got behind the gates withdrew the bolts and the inevitable happened with a number of inmates fleeing. Prisoners and rioters set alight the governor's house, the chapel and the prison's treadmill and gallows. The military was called in to restore order. During the incident about 100 people were killed.

The first of the inner-city riots that occurred in many British cities in the 1980s broke out in the St Paul's suburb. Trouble started after Drug Squad police raided the Black and White Cafe, a known haunt for drug dealers. In the violence that followed, fifty-nine people, most of them police officers, were injured. Twenty-one police vehicles were damaged or destroyed by fire. A post office, bank and several shops were destroyed by fire in the events of April 1980. At one stage eighty police officers faced a crowd of 3,000 rioters.

Thirteen people needed hospital treatment after a bomb explosion, believed to be the work of the Provisional IRA, rocked Park Street in the centre of Bristol on 18 December 1974. Fortunately there was no loss of life although Park Street was busy with late-night Christmas shoppers. The bomb exploded in the doorway of a photographic shop and caused extensive damage to other shops and offices. A man with an Irish accent warned the police in a telephone call about the blast twenty minutes before it happened.

The Provisional IRA also attacked Bristol a week before Christmas in 1978. A bomb of about 5lbs, which had been planted in the foyer of Maggs store in Queens Road, Clifton, exploded in the early hours of Sunday, 17 December. Seven people were injured, mostly by flying glass.

Animal rights activists planted a 5lb bomb in the Senate House, Bristol University's administrative centre, in February 1989. Walls, windows and a ceiling were damaged in the blast just after midnight. No one was hurt. The bomb had been planted in a bar on the fourth floor of the building. Education Secretary Kenneth Baker broke off from a Cabinet meeting in Downing Street to see the damage.

A riot started on the Hartcliffe estate in south Bristol on 16 July 1992 after two men who had stolen an unmarked police motorcycle were killed in a chase with a police patrol car. During the three-day riot, police were stoned and shops in the local shopping centre were destroyed.

An estimated 10,000 people, including children, joined one of the biggest police searches ever known in the Bristol area. They were looking for brother and sister Royston, aged 5, and June Sheasby, aged 7, who left their home on 20 June 1957 to go for a walk but never returned to their family home in Stapleton. Police officers who searched around the clock turned down overtime pay. The bodies of the two children were found ten days later in a shallow grave on the banks of the River Frome at Snuff Mills, not far from their home. Their tiny skulls had been crushed. No one has ever been charged with their murder.

One of the biggest police hunts in the area was launched when the body of 11-year-old Philip Green was found under trees on Shirehampton Golf Course on 31 March 1970. Philip, who lived in nearby Sea Mills, had been collecting lost golf balls which he could sell. He had been hit about the head several times. Despite a major police hunt, which involved house-to-house inquiries in fifty-four streets and thousands of statements taken, Philip's killer has never been found.

More than 16,000 people were questioned after the body of 20-year-old Glenis Carruthers was found on a piece of grassland near Bristol Zoo on a freezing January night in 1974. The student had left a friend's party nearby for fresh air and was never seen alive again. Some seventy people were arrested by the police for questioning but Glenis's killer has never been found.

THE ULTIMATE PENALTY

Sixty-one men and women were hanged between 1752 and 1800 for various crimes they committed in Bristol. This included forging coins, desertion, shoplifting, sinking a ship and stealing linen. One woman was hanged for stealing from prison. Five people were hanged for murder.

Between 1875 and 1963 seventeen people were hanged at Bristol Prison. The eldest was 49 and the youngest was 21. Russell Pascoe, aged 23, was the last person to be executed at the prison. He had an appointment with the hangman on 17 December 1963 for the murder of a farmer in Cornwall. A group of anti-hanging campaigners held a vigil outside the main gates of the prison. They were joined by the Bishop of Bristol, the Rt Revd Oliver Tomkins, who asked the protestors to spare a thought 'for the executioners who have to do this awful job'.

ON A LIGHTER NOTE

For the first time in twenty years no offenders were on the list to appear before Bristol magistrates on 9 September 1916. As was the custom, the court clerk presented the magistrates on duty with a pair of white gloves.

Avon and Somerset Police carried out one of their most unusual investigations after receiving three reports from members of the public of a crocodile swimming in the River Avon near Clifton Suspension Bridge in the summer of 2014. The police said that despite a search for the aquatic reptile nothing was found.

13

THE NATURAL
WORLD

RARE PLANTS PROTECTED

The rare Bristol Onion, or, as it's commonly known because of its shape, the round-head leek, appeared on a postage stamp issued by the Royal Mail in 2009 to highlight endangered plants. The Avon Gorge is the only place in the United Kingdom where the Bristol Onion grows. It was discovered in 1847 and is one of a number of nationally rare or nationally scarce plants that are found in the Avon Gorge.

The Avon Gorge is one of the best-documented botanical sites in Britain with records dating back to 1562. At least twenty-four rare species of plants and trees have been identified on the rockface. Beside the Bristol Onion they include the Bristol Whitebeam, a tree that grows naturally in the Avon Gorge and nowhere else in the world.

Not only is the Avon Gorge a Site of Special Scientific Interest, it is also internationally recognised for the diversity of its flora and fauna. The gorge has been made a Special Area of Conservation under the European Habitats Directive.

Some of the rare plants in the gorge have survived thanks to quick thinking by Isambard Kingdom Brunel, designer of the Clifton Suspension Bridge. When construction work started he was warned that some of the rare plants were at risk of being destroyed. Brunel ordered that the workmen carefully dig up the plants and replant them elsewhere in the gorge.

A herd of goats have been introduced on the Avon Gorge as part of the plan to save rare wild flowers. The six goats have a fenced area of just under 10 acres. They have the task of controlling the scrubby re-growth on the gorge to help restore grass and flowers.

The Avon Gorge, which runs for 1½ miles west of Bristol, forms the boundary between the unitary authorities of Bristol and north Somerset.

More than 4,000 different species of plants can be found in the University of Bristol's Botanic Gardens, which covers a 5-acre site at Stoke Bishop.

ON THE WING

One of the world's most spectacular and fastest birds can be found perched on the top of some of the city's public buildings. The peregrine falcon, which can fly at speeds of up 180mph, is now breeding again in the Avon Gorge after a long absence. Members of the Bristol Ornithological Society have been keeping a 'falcon watch' on the gorge since 1991.

SHEEP ON THE DOWNS

Sheep grazing on Clifton and Durdham Downs was once a familiar sight. An Anglo-Saxon charter of 883 granted grazing rights for the first time. In the nineteenth century there were 2,000 sheep roaming around the grassland. However, grazing died out by 1924 following an outbreak of sheep scab. Earlier there had been complaints from the manager of the Clifton Down Hotel that the bleating of sheep was an annoyance to his guests. Today a number of Downs Commoners still have the right to graze sheep on the Downs and do so occasionally to maintain that tradition.

GEOLOGICAL DIAMONDS

You won't find 'Bristol Diamonds' in any jeweller's shop. Far from being expensive gems the 'diamonds' are multi-faceted quartz crystals found in various parts of the Avon Gorge, including St Vincent's Rocks near the Clifton Suspension Bridge. They were popular as novelties for visitors to the Hotwells Spa in the eighteenth century. Some 2,000 of the crystals were given to King James I as decorations.

Bristol has its own dinosaur called Thecodontosaurus who lived on tropical islands in the Bristol area during the Triassic period around 210 million years ago. Its fossilised bones were found in 1834 in a quarry on Durdham Downs.

ANIMAL MAGIC

Bristol is home to the fifth oldest zoo in the world and the oldest that is not in a capital city. It was opened in July 1836 on 12 acres of farmland on the edge of Clifton Downs and cost £11,372.

The 220 founding shareholders of the zoo included former mayors, councillors and aldermen of Bristol along with businessmen. They included the Duke of Beaufort of Badminton House, South Gloucestershire; Sir John Smyth of Ashton Court; Francis Adams, the former owner of the land; James George, a brewer and representatives of the Fry's (chocolate), Wills (tobacco) and Harford (banking) families. Isambard Kingdom Brunel also bought one share but there is no record of him ever attending a committee meeting.

Some of the zoo's animals were gifts from royalty. Prince Edward, then Prince of Wales, gave a leopard and Queen Victoria presented the zoo with a lioness.

In 1868 the zoo welcomed its first elephant, Zebi, a gift from the Maharajah of Mysore. Zebi was the largest female Asian elephant in captivity at the time and arrived complete with an Indian attendant. The elephant was a popular attraction and became renowned for removing and eating visitors' straw hats.

The zoo advertised itself as 'the finest show in the provinces'. In Victorian days fetes, firework displays and fairground rides were popular as were flower shows and concerts held in the zoo's grounds to raise much-needed funds. There were boat trips on the lake, as well as tennis courts, croquet and archery. Such events were dropped in the 1920s and ever since the zoo has concentrated on research and breeding.

A dozen rhesus monkeys escaped from Bristol Zoo in 1934 when a night-time intruder put a ladder up against their enclosure and released them. It took zookeepers three weeks to recapture them. Some had been found in local gardens and one on the roof of a nearby house.

Rosie the elephant made the headlines when she slowly collapsed whilst carrying ten children around the zoo in the summer of 1947. No one was hurt and Rosie soon got up again. She was given a few days off work to recover and lived for another fourteen years. Zookeepers blamed the hot weather for Rosie's collapse.

The zoo's most popular resident was Alfred the Gorilla, who was an orphan from the African Congo. He was often seen walking around the zoo gardens wearing his trademark cardigan and accompanied by one of his keepers. One of his favourite tricks was to throw snowballs at visitors.

Alfred was so popular that people from all over the world sent him birthday cards every 5 September. It was not his birthday but the anniversary of his arrival at the zoo. Alfred died in 1948 having lived at the zoo for eighteen years. He had been suffering from tuberculosis. Alfred is now embalmed in Bristol Museum and the zoo has a bust of him outside its Ape House.

ANCIENT TREES

Known as the 'Domesday Oak', the oldest tree on the 800-acre Ashton Court estate is thought to be 700 years old. Supporting timbers and wires hold the trunk together, helping it to survive.

About 750 old trees on Clifton and Durdham Downs had to be felled in the 1970s because of the Dutch elm disease that swept across the country.

TALES FROM THE RIVER SEVERN

The River Severn begins in Plynlimon in mid-Wales and finishes at Avonmouth on the edge of Bristol. It is Britain's longest river at 220 miles.

In the winter of 1607 the River Severn froze over, enabling people from the Bristol area to walk across the river to Wales.

The River Severn is almost a mile wide at high water at the point of the first Severn Bridge.

The world-famous Severn Bore occurs when the influx of water from the Atlantic Ocean hits the River Severn's natural flow and creates an extra large wave, much loved by surfboarders.

For centuries baby eels, known as elvers, have been caught in the River Severn by anglers using triangular-shaped nets. The elvers, regarded as a delicacy, were once exported live through Bristol Airport to Europe and Japan to restock the waters.

The tidal range in the Bristol Channel is the second greatest in the world after the Bay of Fundy in Nova Scotia, Canada. The water level in the channel can change by as much as 12m between low and high tide.

UNDER THE WEATHER

Blizzards that swept across the country in the winter of 1881 caused chaos on roads and railways in the West Country. One train that left Temple Meads station at 5.30 p.m. for London did not reach Paddington until 7 p.m. the next day, having been snowed up near Didcot, Wiltshire. The Great Western Railway reported that more than 100 miles of its track were drifted up with sixty-four trains buried in the snow.

Seven ships were stranded in the Avon Gorge because of dense fog blocking the river to other shipping on 1 November 1929. The ships were refloated the next day and the river was back to normal.

The local newspapers reported that on 20 June 1936 Bristol and the surrounding districts experienced what it described as 'the worst electric storm in living memory'. The front-page story of the *Bristol Evening Post* reported that there was 'havoc of thunder, lightning and rain'. Many buildings, including hotels, were struck by lightning and streets were flooded.

Eight lives were lost in Bristol and the West Country in July 1968 when 5in of rain, accompanied by thunder and lightning, swamped the region in twenty-four hours. Emergency accommodation had to be found for hundreds of families in south Bristol while floodwater was pumped from their homes. In some cases floodwater had reached bedroom level and some families were rescued by rowing boat.

The freak storm brought production at the Wills tobacco factory at Bedminster to a halt. Some 50 million cigarettes and 210,000 tons of tobacco in cartons ready to be distributed to retailers were damaged by floodwater and had to be dumped on a council refuse tip at Lawrence Weston.

As the River Chew at Pensford, a few miles south of Bristol, burst its banks the stone bridge collapsed. Soldiers from the Royal Engineers were called in to erect a temporary Bailey bridge across the river.

The 1968 storm was said to have been the worst in the area for more than fifty years and was called by the newspapers 'the Great Flood'.

During the drought in the summer of 1976 it was so hot that the daytime temperature in Bristol never dropped below 70 degrees Fahrenheit between 22 June and 20 July.

Bristol Waterworks reported that it was losing nearly 6 million gallons of water a day from their reservoirs through evaporation. This was twice as much as in a normal summer.

Chew Valley Reservoir, which supplies thousands of homes in north Somerset and Bristol, dried out exposing the village that was submerged when the lake was created.

Health inspectors condemned more than 1,500 carcasses of lamb from New Zealand that arrived at Avonmouth Docks. The lamb was due for delivery to wholesale butchers in the Bristol area but the inspectors ruled that although the carcasses had travelled in a refrigerated ship the hot weather had still managed to make the meat unfit to be sold.

The hot weather jammed the Cumberland Basin Swing Bridge. When the bridge refused to swing to allow shipping into the City Docks, council workmen were called in to hose it down with cold water.

The drought meant that ice cream makers had never had such a good time. One Bristol family business with several ice cream parlours in the city rationed the number of ice cream cones and wafers customers could buy because of the huge demand for them.

The drought, which started in June, came to a sudden end in the last days of August with violent thunderstorms.

14

SPORTING BRISTOL

SPORTING HEROES

Dr William Grace (1848–1915) is best remembered for his cricketing skills rather than those with the stethoscope. He was born into a cricketing family at Downend, just over the Bristol boundary in what is now South Gloucestershire. Grace was regarded as a 'champion' and the greatest player the game had ever produced. He played for Gloucestershire and was selected for England twenty-two times. During his career Grace made 126 centuries, scored 54,896 runs and took nearly 3,000 wickets.

Arthur Milton from Bedminster was the last man to play both football and cricket for England. As a cricketer he played for Gloucestershire from 1948–74, captaining the county in 1968. He also played in six test matches for England. Milton scored a total of 32,150 first class runs. As a footballer he turned out for Arsenal between 1951–55 and made 84 appearances for the club. He got the ball into the net 21 times. Milton was capped by England once in 1951. He played for Bristol City in 1955 before retiring from the game later that year. He died in 2007 aged 79.

Jo Durie, who was born in Bristol in 1960 and went to Clifton High School, was ranked as Britain's top female tennis player at the age of 23. She was also singles world number five professional tennis player and reached the quarter-finals at Wimbledon in 1984. She retired from playing in 1995 and went into coaching.

HIGHS AND LOWS OF
BRISTOL CITY FOOTBALL CLUB

Bristol City started life as Bristol South End in 1894 and played at St John's Lane, Bedminster. A Bristol South End street nameplate, off St John's Lane, today recalls the club's early times. In 1897 the club renamed itself as Bristol City and three years later it merged with Bedminster Football Club who played at Ashton Gate. This ground became the permanent home of the merged club from 1904.

The club lost a lot of 'gate' money when it played at St John's Lane as fans climbed a nearby hill to watch matches free of charge. Not to be beaten, the football club erected hoardings 30ft high that blocked the view.

Bristol City was admitted to the Football League in 1901 and its first game was an away fixture to Blackpool which City won 2–0.

The club's first game at Ashton Gate saw Bolton Wanderers defeat the home side 4–3. The match attracted about 14,000 spectators.

The club's highest-ever score in the Football Association Cup was in November 1960 when it beat Chichester City 11–0 in the first round of the competition.

Bristol City reached the final of the FA Cup in 1909 when it played Manchester United at Crystal Palace. Watched by 74,401 spectators, United won the match 1–0. It is the first and only time so far that a football club from Bristol has reached the Cup Final.

City's biggest league win was a 9–0 victory over Aldershot in December 1946 when both clubs were in Division Three (South).

City's biggest defeat ever was at the hands of Coventry City in April 1934. The Midlands club won the match 9–0.

An all-time record of 43,335 spectators packed Ashton Gate Stadium for City's Fifth Round FA Cup match against Preston North End in 1935. The game ended in a goalless draw. Preston won the replay 5–0.

Bristol City's directors were so keen for the club to be promoted that when they appointed Alan Dicks manager in October 1967 his contract included bonuses if he succeeded. He would get an extra £5,000 if he took the club up to the First Division but only £1,000 if City stayed in Division Two.

In 1982 Bristol City, then playing in Division Four, faced major financial difficulties. This led to eight of the club's highest earners from the days when they were in Division One tearing up their contracts to alleviate the situation. The eight agreed to terminate their contracts for half the fee. This ensured that the club could survive and was reformed as Bristol City (1982) Football Club. The eight players – Julian Marshall, David Rodgers, Gerry Sweeney, Chris Garland, Jimmy Mann, Trevor Tainton, Peter Aitken and Geoff Merrick – were inevitably dubbed by the press as the 'Ashton Gate Eight'.

SOME BRISTOL CITY STARS

Billy 'Fatty' Wedlock is still talked about today even though he played for Bristol City between 1900–22, having joined the club when he was 20 years old. During most of his career he skippered the side and made 364 appearances in league matches. He was selected to play for England 26 times. On his retirement Billy took over the pub opposite the main gates of Bristol City's stadium. It was then known as the *Star* but its name was later changed to Wedlock's in Billy's honour. He died in 1965 aged 83.

Bristol City striker Don Clark holds the club record for scoring the most goals in one season. Clark (1917–2014) netted the ball 42 times in the 1946/47 season. It is a club record that has never been equalled or surpassed.

Chris Garland, who lived in a multi-storey block of flats overlooking Bristol City's stadium, achieved a long-held ambition to play for the club when he signed a contract with them in 1965. He stayed with the club until 1971 when he was sold to Chelsea for £100,000, a record fee at the time for either of the city's two league clubs. Garland rejoined City in 1976 and stayed with the club until 1983.

FIVE FAMOUS BRISTOL CITY SUPPORTERS

Jenson Button, Formula 1 racing driver.
John Cleese, actor who appeared in *Monty Python* and *Fawlty Towers*.
Tony Robinson, actor who starred in *Blackadder*.
The Wurzels, the West Country's self-styled 'Scrumpy and Western' band.
Banksy, graffiti artist.

NON-SPORTING EVENTS AT BRISTOL CITY'S STADIUM

Nearly a quarter of a million people went through the turnstiles at City's Ashton Gate Stadium in May 1984. But they were not there to see a football match. They turned up to see the American evangelist Billy Graham who took over the stadium for a week-long series of religious revival rallies. The rallies were so popular that coaches ferried people from all over the West Country and South Wales to Ashton Gate.

The goal nets at Ashton Gate were dismantled in 1982 for the first of a series of major name rock and pop concerts staged at City's ground. The inaugural concert starred the Rolling Stones who attracted 36,000 fans. The concert was part of the band's world tour.

A concert by Canadian singer Bryan Adams in May 2003 attracted 19,000 fans.

In June 2004 Sir Elton John was watched by 22,000 fans at a concert at Ashton Gate.

In 2008 the American rock band Bon Jovi attracted an audience of 24,000 people at Ashton Gate.

The Irish boy band Westlife performed in front of a crowd of 15,000 people when they played at the stadium in 2010.

HIGHS AND LOWS FOR
BRISTOL ROVERS FOOTBALL CLUB

A football club called the Black Arabs, later to be known as Bristol Rovers, was formed at a meeting in a restaurant on Stapleton Road in 1883. Their name came from the fact that their kit was mainly black and they played on a neighbouring pitch to the Arabs rugby team at Purdown.

The Black Arabs' first match was in December 1883 when the side took on Wotton-under-Edge. This was a friendly game which the Gloucestershire team won 6–1.

Bristol Rovers played under that name for the first time in 1898. By then they were playing at Eastville Stadium, which was to be their home for nearly a century. The club bought the ground in 1921 but sold it nineteen years later to the Bristol Greyhound Company through which they rented the stadium for the rest of the club's time there.

Bristol Rovers played their last game at Eastville on 26 April 1986 drawing 1–1 against Chesterfield in front of a crowd of 3,576 fans.

From 1986 the club shared Bath City's ground at Twerton Park for the next ten years. From 1996 onwards the club shared the Memorial Ground at Filton with Bristol Rugby Club. However, at the start of the 2014–15 season the rugby club moved to Ashton Gate Stadium to ground share with Bristol City.

Bristol Rovers suffered its worst defeat when Luton Town beat them 12–0 in a Division 3 South match in 1936.

The number seven seems to have been a lucky one for the club. Rovers beat Brighton and Hove Albion 7–0 in November 1952, defeated Swansea City 7–0 in October 1954 and Shrewsbury Town 7–0 in March 1964.

A record home attendance was recorded on 30 January 1960 when Rovers entertained Preston North End in the FA Cup. A total of 38,472 spectators went through the turnstiles.

Bristol Rovers were admitted to the Football League in August 1920. Their first match in the league was against Millwall which they lost 2–0. Rovers were relegated from the Football League for the first time in ninety-four years when they lost 1–0 to Mansfield Town on the last day of the League Two season at the end of the 2013–14 season.

LONGEST-SERVING
BRISTOL ROVERS MANAGERS

Alfred Homer was appointed Rovers' first full-time manager-secretary. He took up the post in 1899 and held it for twenty-one years. Brough Fletcher became manager in 1938 and served the club for twelve years.

Bert Tann, who was the club's coach, succeeded Brough to become Rover's longest-serving post-war manager. He was appointed to the managerial role in 1950 and served the club for eighteen years in the post.

ENGLAND STAR SIGNS
FOR BRISTOL ROVERS

Alan Ball, who played for England in the World Cup-winning side in 1966, played for Rovers between 1982–83. He made 17 appearances for the club and scored 2 goals.

YOUNGEST GOAL SCORER

Ronnie Dix, a professional footballer with Bristol Rovers, made history in March 1928 by becoming the youngest goal scorer in Football League history. In a Third Division (South) match against Norwich he scored a goal when he was just 15 years and 180 days old. His goal helped Rovers win the match 3–0.

FIVE FAMOUS BRISTOL ROVERS SUPPORTERS

Jeffrey Archer, Lord Archer of Weston-super-Mare, former Member of Parliament and novelist.
Rod Hull, the comedian best known for his puppet Emu.
Roni Size, musician and Mercury prize-winner.
David Graveney, former chairman of the England Test selectors and ex-Gloucestershire Country Cricket club player.
David 'Syd' Lawrence, former England and Gloucestershire cricketer.

NON-FOOTBALL EVENTS AT EASTVILLE STADIUM

Greyhound racing started at the stadium in 1932 with the last race meeting taking place in 1997.

The stadium was also the home of Bristol Bulldogs Speedway team who raced there in the 1970s.

Eastville Stadium was demolished in 1998 to make way for a supermarket.

Bristol Rovers' ground was probably the only one in the country with flowerbeds behind the goals.

FOOTBALL ON THE DOWNS

Since 1905 organised football matches have been played on Clifton and Durdham Downs under the auspices of the Downs League. This is a standalone league that does not feed into the English Football League system. Every Saturday more than fifty teams play in four divisions on the Downs involving more than 500 players and officials. It is believed to be the only league in the country that plays all its matches at the same time and same place.

THE SPORT OF KINGS

One of Bristol's most popular sporting activities in the eighteenth and nineteenth centuries was the annual horseracing that was staged each spring on an improvised course on the Downs from around 1718. The Durdham Down Races attracted great crowds, traders' stalls and marquees. There were trophies and cash prizes for the winning horses and jockeys, sometimes as much as 100 sovereigns.

Families promenading on Durdham Downs in July 1785 witnessed a rather strange equestrian event. A local paper reported that 'Thomas Jefferson rode two horses at full speed with a foot on each of their backs and afterwards rode 100 yards standing on his head'. Due to so much interest from the public Mr Jefferson repeated his stunt two days later.

A racecourse opened at Knowle in March 1873 under the patronage of the Prince of Wales. The first three-day meeting, which included steeple chasing and flat racing, attracted more than 200,000 spectators with the Prince of Wales attending each day.

The main race of the meeting was the Bristol Grand Steeplechase with a £500 prize for the winner. Due to financial problems the racecourse closed in 1878 and the site eventually became the home of Knowle Golf Club, which still exists.

STORIES ABOUT THE OVAL BALL

Rugby Union players in Bristol who lost their lives in the Great War are remembered at the Memorial Stadium on Filton Avenue, which is dedicated to them. The Lord Mayor officially opened it in 1921 and immediately afterwards the first match kicked off with Bristol beating Cardiff by 18 points to 3 points. The ground became the home of Bristol Rugby Club, which had played on various pitches around the city since its formation in 1888.

New Zealand All Blacks played Bristol Rugby Club and won 41–1 during a tour of the UK in 1905. The match was played at the County Ground, headquarters of Gloucestershire County Cricket Club.

Four members of Bristol Ladies Rugby Team – Sophie Hemming, 34; Amber Reed, 23; Kay Wilson, 22 and Danielle Waterman, 29 – were in the England team that beat Canada in the Women's World Championship in Paris in 2014.

Little could the group of men who met in the King's Arms on Whiteladies Road in the autumn of 1872 realise that they were making sporting history. They formed Clifton Rugby Club, which is Bristol's oldest rugby club. Clifton RFC is also the twentieth oldest club in England. It still retains its amateur status and was instrumental in the creation of the game as it evolved in the late nineteenth century.

DANGEROUS SPORTS

The first modern bungee jump was made by members of Oxford University's Dangerous Sports Club when they visited Bristol on 1 April 1979. In one of their most daring stunts four members of the club jumped off Clifton Suspension Bridge with nothing between it and the River Avon 245ft below. The students used 2in-thick elasticated ropes that they had attached to themselves and the bridge structure. Fortunately, the four men, who even enjoyed a champagne toast dangling halfway down the Avon Gorge, came to no harm. The bridge authorities alerted the police who took the men to a police station for questioning.

MEDAL WINNERS

Not only did Robin Cousins pick up a gold medal for ice skating in the Winter Olympics at Lake Placid in America in 1980 but on his return to Britain he was the subject of the television programme *This Is Your Life*. It was a closely guarded secret that Cousins, from Sea Mills, would be on the programme until its presenter Eamonn Andrews 'pounced' on him as he was being congratulated by the Lord Mayor of Bristol in front of thousands of supporters on College Green. Cousins was then taken to the HTV studios at Arnos Vale for the recording of the programme.

Former chalet maid Jenny Jones aged 34 from Downend, now a professional snowboarder, became the first Briton to win an Olympic medal in a snow event. She collected a bronze medal in slope-style in the 2014 Winter Olympics at Socchi.

Sixteen-year-old artistic gymnast Claudia Fragapane from Longwell Green won four gold medals at the 2014 Commonwealth Games in Glasgow. Claudia, who was dubbed by the newspapers as the 'pocket rocket' on account of her height of 4ft 6in, was the first Englishwoman for eighty-four years to win four gold medals at a Commonwealth Games. She started training when she was just 6 years old. At the same Commonwealth Games David Luckman, 38 from Clifton, became a double gold medallist in shooting.

POWERBOATS IN THE DOCKS

The City Docks gave way to powerboat racing from 1972 until 1990. Drivers from all over the world raced around the course at speeds in excess of 80mph. Each year the weekend of powerboat racing attracted more than 20,000 spectators who lined the quayside for the spills and thrills. The racing came to an end after a number of drivers were either killed or injured.

HALF MARATHON RUNNERS

The Lord Mayor, Councillor Alastair Watson, took part in the 2014 Bristol Half Marathon wearing his heavy, red wool and fake fur mayoral gown, tricorn hat and chain of office. Mr Watson, aged 58, is no stranger to the race, having run in it ten times before. He covered the course in 2014 in two hours, one minute and eleven seconds.

Bristol's half marathon has been staged since 1989 with the first event attracting just 1,000 runners. In 2014 there were 8,000 runners, some of them coming from overseas. They ran a sea-level route that takes them past the old City Docks, out and back along the Portway Road before returning to the city centre.

For the first time since it was opened in 1966 the first Severn Bridge (M48) was closed to traffic on 24 August 2014 for the inaugural Severn Bridge Half Marathon.

Around 2,000 runners took part, starting at the Chepstow end of the bridge, running across it and then pounding the roads around South Gloucestershire before returning across the bridge to Chepstow.

CITY ON TWO WHEELS

Bristol was named by the government as the first 'Cycling City' in England in 2008. It gave the council £11 million to encourage more cycling by creating cycle lanes and providing more cycle training for children.

Sir Bradley Wiggins and 107 other top cyclists took to some of Bristol's steepest hills when the fourth stage of the Friends Life Tour of Britain cycle race reached the city in the autumn of 2014. The route included Bridge Valley Road, which rises more than 200ft from The Portway to Clifton Downs. Bristol was the halfway point of the eight-day race, which started in Liverpool and finished in London.

SPORTING SNIPPETTS

In the late eighteenth and early nineteenth centuries bare-knuckle fighting was a big spectator sport with training and matches taking place at the Hatchet Inn in Frogmore Street. One of the most popular fighters was Tom Cribb from Hanham who held the national title of Champion Prize Fighter for nine years. He had only one defeat in thirty major fights. Cribb is said to have often walked 100 miles before a fight in order to lose weight.

Round-the-world yachtsman Tony Bullimore from Westbury Park thought his career was nearly over when his yacht capsized in the Southern Ocean, some 2,500 miles off the south-west coast of Australia. Fortunately for Bullimore he was trapped in an air pocket under the hull. Rescuers reached him four days after the dramatic incident, which made worldwide headlines on radio, television and in newspapers. It happened while he was taking part in the 1996 Vendee Globe single-handed around-the-world race.

After hanging up his football boots for the last time with Bristol Rovers, former captain Geoff Twentyman joined BBC Radio Bristol, initially in the station's sports department, but he has since become an evening 'Drive-Time' programme presenter. Twentyman was with Rovers from 1986 to 1993 and made 252 appearances for the club. Before joining them he had played for Preston North End.

Cricketing history was made in 1862 when Gloucestershire County Cricket Club played what was probably their first county match on the pitch of Clifton Cricket Club on The Downs, which had been in use since 1835. The Gentlemen of Gloucestershire beat the Gentlemen of Devonshire by an innings and 77 runs.

The biggest cricket score in the world involved a 13-year-old schoolboy. In 1899 Arthur Collins scored 628 runs not out in a school match at Clifton College. He was at the crease for five days and knocked up the remarkable score. There was immense interest in Master Collins' feat with even *The Times* running a headline that said: 'Collins Still In'. Despite the passage of time Collins' score has never been equalled or surpassed by any professional or amateur player in the world.

Clifton Suspension Bridge was closed to traffic as the London 2012 Olympics flame was carried across it on its way to the capital during the morning traffic rush hour. As the torch-bearers ran cross the bridge, streamers were released and fireworks exploded.

15

ON
THIS DAY

1 January 2000   Peter Rew and Margaret Hornsby made history by being the first couple to marry in Bristol in the new millennium. They walked down the aisle at St Philip and Jacob church, Old Market.

2 January 1950   Bert Tann was appointed manager of Bristol Rovers, a post he held for eighteen years.

3 January 1941   The clock at Temple Meads railway station, which had long been a landmark, was destroyed in an air raid.

4 January 1999   Dawn Primarolo, MP for Bristol South, was appointed Paymaster General.

6 January 1991   Bristol band Massive Attack launched their first album *Blue Lines*.

7 January 1956   Bristol Rovers beat Manchester United 4–0 watched by 35,872 spectators at Eastville Stadium.

8 January 1823   A Welsh Congregational chapel opened on Lower Castle Street.

9 January 1907   Henleaze Congregational church opened at a cost of £7,000.

10 January 1784   An unmanned hydrogen balloon flew from Bath to Bristol.

11 January 1955	The BBC took over the Empire Theatre, Old Market.
12 January 1897	Two men lost their lives when fire destroyed the *Xema* steamer in Cumberland Basin.
13 January 1881	Blizzards hit the West Country. It took one train twenty hours to travel from Bristol to London.
14 January 1958	Bert Tann, Bristol Rovers manager, was the first local person to appear on Television Wales and West (TWW), which went on air on this date.
15 January 1859	An African trading ship, the *Porto Novo*, was destroyed by fire while unloading in Redcliffe Wharf.
16 January 1820	The Floating Harbour froze over as the temperature fell to -24° Fahrenheit.
17 January 1887	An experimental street lighting scheme using arc lamps started in the centre of the city for a month.
18 January 1904	Archibald Leach, who became Hollywood film star Cary Grant, was born in Horfield.
19 January 1972	The Theatre Royal reopened after a twenty-month refit that included a new facade and foyer.
20 January 1838	Twenty-nine passengers and crew perished when their steamboat on its way from Cork to Bristol was wrecked in a gale.
21 January 1976	Both the English and French-built Concorde aircraft made their first commercial flights.
25 January 1869	Charles Dickens read from his books *David Copperfield* and *Pickwick Papers* at the Victoria Rooms.

27 January 1962   The *Bristol Evening World* was published for the last time after thirty-three years. Its circulation had dropped from 80,000 to about 30,000.

28 January 1889   Four miners lost their lives in an explosion at Dean Lane Colliery, Southville.

29 January 1712   The Congress of Utrecht opened with the Bishop of Bristol, the Rt Revd John Robinson, representing Britain. It resulted in the Treaty of Utrecht that ended the war of the Spanish succession.

31 January 1983   BBC's *Animal Magic*, broadcast from Bristol studios, went on air for the last time after twenty-one years.

2 February 1745   Hannah More, who was to become a noted philanthropist, writer and social reformer, was born in Fishponds.

3 February 1821   Elizabeth Blackwell, who became the first woman in the world to qualify as a doctor, was born in St Paul's.

4 February 1954   A Bristol Britannia aircraft on a test flight from Filton airfield crashed on to Littleton Mudflats, Severn Estuary. The aircraft was destroyed but no one was seriously injured.

5 February 1945   More than 100 firefighters tackled a blaze that destroyed the Colston Hall. It was believed to have been caused by a discarded cigarette.

6 February 1966   Whiteladies Cinema became the first cinema in Bristol to have licensed bars.

9 February 1940   George VI made a seven-hour visit to Bristol to see the city's 'war effort'.

10 February 1824   Samuel Plimsoll, inventor of a safety loading line for ships, was born at Redcliffe.

14 February 1807   Eight people were fined by magistrates for not sweeping the pathway outside their homes.

15 February 1965   The area finals of the 'Miss England' beauty contest planned to be held at a club in Clifton were cancelled because there were only two contestants.

17 February 1832   Holy Trinity church, the first church in the St Philips area, was opened at a cost of £9,000.

18 February 1904   A group of artists calling themselves the Bristol Savages was established. They still meet during the winter.

19 February 1946   The curtain went up on Bristol Old Vic Theatre Company's first season at the Theatre Royal with a production of Farquhar's *The Beau Stratagem*.

20 February 1905   Bristol Art Gallery opened. The gallery had nearly 300,000 visitors in its first three months.

21 February 1980   Robin Cousins, aged 23, from Sea Mills, won a gold medal for figure skating at the Winter Olympics in Lake Placid, America.

23 February 1952   Nearly 1,000 people packed Bristol Cathedral for a midday memorial service commemorating George VI who died earlier in the month.

24 February 1955   The American jazz vocalist Ella Fitzgerald appeared at the Colston Hall.

25 February 2005   The queen opened Bristol University's Laboratory for Advanced Dynamics (BLADE) which cost £18.5 million.

26 February 1861   The City and County of Bristol Lunatic Asylum opened with room for 200 patients.

27 February 1961	Rosemary Frankland, the reigning 'Miss World' who represented Wales, attracted crowds on a visit to Bristol.
2 March 1967	About 2,000 students at Bristol Technical College, Ashley Down, boycotted its refectory complaining about the quality and prices of meals and its opening hours.
3 March 1965	The Princess Royal opened a new terminal at Bristol Airport.
4 March 1905	A statue of a soldier with a rifle was unveiled outside the Victoria Rooms, Clifton, as a memorial to the Gloucestershire Regiment.
5 March 1837	Four people lost their lives in a fire at the William IV tavern, Temple Street.
6 March 1967	Some 500 students taking part in a twenty-four-hour pedal car race on the site of the old Whitchurch Airport were treated for ammonia burns to their hands, faces and eyes.
7 March 1833	Isambard Kingdom Brunel, who was already working on Clifton Suspension Bridge, was appointed engineer of the Bristol committee of the Great Western Railway.
8 March 2002	Prince Philip visited the Society of Merchant Venturers to help celebrate the organisation's 450th anniversary.
10 March 1801	Bristol's population in the first National Census was counted at 68,000.
12 March 2004	Baroness Hale was installed as the seventh chancellor of Bristol University.
13 March 1970	Bristol businessman Tom King was elected MP for Bridgwater at a by-election. Mr King, who held the seat for the Conservative Party for thirty-one years, was made a life peer in 2001.

14 March 1911   The War Office placed its first order for
the Bristol-built Boxkite aircraft.

15 March 1980   The Gaumont Cinema, Baldwin Street,
closed after nearly 100 years as
a variety theatre or cinema.

18 March 1901   The first bananas to be seen in the
West Country arrived at Avonmouth
Docks. More than 18,000 tons of them
had been shipped in from Jamaica.

19 March 1873   Knowle Racecourse opened in the
presence of the Prince of Wales.

21 March 1590   Queen Elizabeth I granted a charter to
Queen Elizabeth Hospital, which formally
set up the boys' school following an
endowment by soap merchant John Carr.

23 March 1811   A riot broke out in Bristol Market because
fresh butter had increased in price.

25 March 1970   A salvage team arrived in the Falkland
Islands to bring the hulk of Brunel's SS *Great
Britain* back to Bristol for restoration.

26 March 1897   Bristol Rovers Football Club was registered
as a Public Liability Company.

27 March 1905   The first meeting of the Downs Football
League took place with three divisions
of ten teams playing on the same site.

29 March 1787   Pioneering chocolate maker Joseph Fry
died in Bristol aged 59. His business
continued to be run by the Fry family.

1 April 1974   Bristol became part of the new Avon
County. Twenty-two years later it was
abolished and Bristol reverted to its
former City and County of Bristol status.

2 April 2003	Businessman Jack Hayward, who funded the return of the SS *Great Britain* from the Falkland Islands to Bristol in 1970, was granted the Freedom of Bristol.
8 April 1838	Brunel's SS *Great Western* left Avonmouth for America with seven passengers on board for its maiden voyage.
10 April 1973	Some 108 people, mostly women, were killed when a plane that left Bristol Airport on a day's shopping trip to Switzerland ploughed into a snowy hillside on its landing approach at Basle.
11 April 1148	St Augustine's Abbey (later to become Bristol Cathedral) was formally dedicated.
12 April 1935	The Bristol Blenheim light bomber aircraft, designed and built at Filton, made its first flight.
17 April 1956	The queen opened the Council House (now City Hall) at College Green, the administrative headquarters of Bristol City Council.
18 April 1932	The first edition of the *Bristol Evening Post* appeared as a twenty-four-page paper.
21 April 1979	Concorde 216, the last supersonic aircraft to be built at Filton, made its maiden flight.
22 April 1972	Concorde 002 made its first appearance in Germany, at the Hanover Air Show.
1 May 1957	The Duchess of Kent opened the new Bristol (Lulsgate) Airport that replaced the original civil airport at Whitchurch.
2 May 2003	The Labour Party was swept from power on Bristol City Council after nearly thirty years. The results of the local elections meant that no political party was left with an overall majority.

4 May 1997   Dawn Primarolo, MP for Bristol South, was appointed Secretary of the Treasury.

5 May 1974   'Scrumpy and Western' singer Adge Cutler died in a road accident near Chepstow on his way home from appearing at a concert in Hereford.

6 May 1949   A Bristol Freighter aircraft on a test flight from Filton crashed into the sea off Portland Bill, Dorset, killing all seven people on board.

9 May 1728   Princess Amelia, daughter of George III, visited the city. She travelled from London to Bath in a sedan chair and made the rest of the journey by boat.

10 May 1957   Princess Margaret visited Hartcliffe housing estate in south Bristol and opened Hareclive Primary School.

12 May 1966   Fire ripped through the Co-op's multi-storey Fairfax House store on the edge of Broadmead shopping centre.

13 May 1999   Courage Brewery announced that it was to close its brewery in Bath Street. Beer had been brewed on the site for nearly 300 years.

15 May 1944   The last entry in the official Bristol Blitz diary records that ten high-explosive incendiaries fell on various parts of the city.

17 May 1861   The Royal Assent was given to the Clifton and Durdham Downs Act of Parliament which ensures that 440 acres of wooded and open country 'shall for ever hereafter be kept open and unenclosed as a place of public resort'.

19 May 1966   The Mecca organisation opened a £32 million entertainments complex in Frogmore Street. It included a dozen bars, an ice rink, bowling lanes, casino, nightclub, ballroom and cinema.

20 May 1994	The Duke of Edinburgh laid the keel of a replica of the *Matthew* in which explorer John Cabot sailed from Bristol and discovered Newfoundland.
24 May 1842	The Victoria Rooms, Clifton, built at a cost of nearly £30,000 as a venue for meetings and concerts, opened four years to the day after its foundation stone was laid. It is now the home of Bristol University's music department.
25 May 1787	Avonmouth Lighthouse came into service for the first time. The light from its 85ft-high tower could be seen 14 miles out at sea.
26 May 1982	Statues of Isambard Kingdom Brunel were unveiled in Bristol city centre and at Paddington station.
30 May 1988	Warehouses at Canons Marsh used as Customs and Excise tobacco bonds were demolished in a controlled explosion to make way for regeneration of the City Docks.
1 June 1927	The Bristol and District Employment Committee announced that 14,822 people were out of work.
2 June 1972	The Bristol-built Concorde 002 left England for a sales demonstration tour of twelve countries in the Middle East and Australia.
3 June 1919	The first sod of earth was cut for the new Sea Mills housing estate, which was dubbed Bristol's first 'Garden City'. The first homes were ready for occupation within a year.
4 June 1846	Fire destroyed a sugar refinery at Counterslip causing damage of £40,000.
7 June 1851	Eight men were killed when a steam boiler exploded at the Starve-all Colliery, St George.

8 June 1868	The Bishop of Bristol and Gloucester consecrated All Saints church, Clifton, although it was another four years before building work was completed.
9 June 1925	King George V and Queen Mary opened the Wills Memorial Building, which is part of Bristol University's campus. The king used a specially carved key to unlock the doors.
10 June 1938	The Duchess of Beaufort laid the foundation stone of the Council House, College Green. Work on Bristol City Council's administrative headquarters was held up by the Second World War.
18 June 1912	King George V and Queen Mary officially opened the King Edward VII Memorial Infirmary on Lower Maudlin Street.
21 June 1831	The foundation stone of the Clifton Suspension Bridge at the Clifton end was laid watched by Isambard Kingdom Brunel.
24 June 1899	The first underground toilet in the city was opened in St Nicholas Street.
25 June 1542	Paul Bush was consecrated the first Bishop of Bristol.
26 June 1956	Dame Sybil Thorndike and Sir Lewis Casson opened Bristol Old Vic Theatre School at Downside, Clifton. It replaced the original school in King Street.
28 June 1879	Portishead Dock, covering 12 acres of land owned by Bristol Corporation, was opened.
29 June 1927	About 1,000 people gathered on Observatory Hill, Clifton, to witness a partial eclipse of the sun at 6.15 a.m.

1 July 1995	The queen opened a new extension at Bristol Dental Hospital.
4 July 1913	King George V unveiled a bronze statue of his father, Edward VII, outside the Victoria Rooms, Clifton.
5 July 1970	The SS *Great Britain* passed under the Clifton Suspension Bridge, both built by Brunel, on her way back to her original berth in Bristol Docks for restoration.
8 July 1908	King Edward VII opened the Royal Edward Dock, Avonmouth.
9 July 1878	The Royal Agricultural Society's show held on Clifton and Durdham Downs attracted 121,851 visitors.
16 July 1846	Bristol Waterworks Company was established by an Act of Parliament.
19 July 1970	The SS *Great Britain* returned to her original berth in Bristol City Docks with Prince Philip on board. This was the last leg of the journey from the Falkland Islands.
22 July 1849	Twenty-one people were killed or injured when the *Red Rover* steamboat exploded in the Floating Harbour.
23 July 1927	Knowle Greyhound Racing Stadium opened with more than 7,000 first-night spectators.
24 July 1985	Gloucestershire County Cricket Club welcomed the Australian cricket team at the start of a three-day match. Australia won the game by 170 runs.
27 July 1816	The Duke of Wellington was granted the Freedom of Bristol by the mayor at a special ceremony hosted by the city council.

1 August 1922	A combined swimming pool and cinema was opened on Gloucester Road. Silent films were screened in winter and in summer the floorboards were removed to provide the pool.
2 August 1784	The first mail coach on the Bristol–London route set out from High Street.
5 August 1973	Bristol Rovers won the Watney Cup by 7 goals to 6 against Sheffield United in a penalty shoot-out.
6 August 1497	Church bells rang out to welcome the return of explorer John Cabot who sailed from Bristol and made landfall at Newfoundland.
9 August 1973	The queen spent a day in Bristol as part of her Jubilee tour. Her visit coincided with celebrations marking Bristol's 600th anniversary as a county.
12 August 1877	The last service was held at St Werburgh's church, Corn Street, before the church was taken down and rebuilt a couple of miles away.
13 August 1930	The city's first traffic lights were switched on at the junction of Whiteladies Road and Tyndalls Park Road, Clifton.
14 August 1574	Queen Elizabeth I started a six-day visit to Bristol which cost the Corporation £1,053 14*s* 11*d*. As part of the entertainment laid on for her a mock river battle took place in the River Avon.
15 August 1348	The Black Death broke out in Bristol, eventually causing the death of about a third of the town's population.
20 August 1963	A by-election in the Bristol South-East constituency saw the return to the House of Commons by Tony Benn. He had renounced the peerage he had inherited and stood for re-election.

21 August 1743	The Exchange, Corn Street, built by John Wood the Elder, was opened amidst much ceremony. A 2-mile-long procession of civic dignitaries and forty-eight private carriages, accompanied by the roar of canons, processed through the centre of the city.
23 August 2002	Prime Minister Tony Blair's office confirmed that his son Euan Blair had won a place at Bristol University to study ancient history.
24 August 1970	The tug *Varius* began its 8,000-mile journey towing the hulk of the SS *Great Britain* from the Falkland Islands to Bristol.
26 August 1868	Work started on building Avonmouth Dock.
27 August 1991	Bristol City Council sold the Port of Bristol to a private operator in a £36 million deal.
30 August 1879	The first service was held in St Werburgh's church after it was rebuilt stone by stone.
31 August 1891	Ten miners were killed in an explosion at the Malago coal pit.
1 September 1895	Fire destroyed the first Salvation Army chapel built in Bristol at Stokes Croft.
4 September 1949	The Brabazon aircraft, at the time the world's biggest plane, made its maiden flight over Bristol.
5 September 2007	One of Bristol's best-known hotels, the Avon Gorge, standing next to the Clifton Suspension Bridge, was sold for £15.5 million. It was bought by the Hong Kong and London-based Swire Group.
6 September 1690	William III arrived at King Road near Avonmouth on his victorious return from the Battle of the Boyne. He was visiting his Irish Secretary of State who lived at Kings Weston House, Shirehampton.

8 September 1996   The queen opened the Severn Bridge
linking England with Wales.

10 September 1886   Eight miners were killed in an explosion at Dean
Lane Colliery, Southville. The coroner's report said
the men had been using naked flames to light the pit.

12 September 1687   King James II visited Bristol with his queen.

15 September 1859   Isambard Kingdom Brunel died aged 53.
He was buried at Kensal Green cemetery, London.

18 September 1934   The BBC studios in Whiteladies Road were
officially opened by the Lord Mayor.

20 September 1971   Concorde 001, the first pre-production
aircraft, was rolled out at Filton.

21 September 1967   An Aer Lingus aircraft over-ran the runway at
Bristol Airport on arrival from Dublin. No one
was injured but the plane was written-off.

23 September 1844   Brunel's SS *Great Britain* ran aground at
Dundrum Bay, County Down, Northern
Ireland. It spent almost a year there before
being towed to Liverpool Docks.

26 September 1965   The Rolling Stones appeared before a full house
of 2,000 fans at the Colston Hall. The concert
was part of the group's national tour.

27 September 1847   Two members of the Wills tobacco family –
George Alfred and Henry Herbert – were
granted the Freedom of Bristol at a
special meeting of the city council.

29 September 1811   The first club for businessmen in the city,
the Commercial Rooms, opened in Corn Street.
It was converted into a pub in 1995.

30 September 1957   Kudos and Kylow, two German Shepherd
Alsatians, went on duty as the first police
dogs recruited by Bristol Constabulary.

3 October 1818   The Clifton Club was founded at a meeting presided over by Sir Richard Vaughan, a former Mayor of Bristol. It was originally a men-only club but there are now women members.

4 October 1795   The poet Samuel Taylor Coleridge married Sarah Fricker at St Mary Redcliffe church.

9 October 1906   Fire destroyed the Society of Merchant Venturers Technical College in Unity Street.

10 October 1854   Social reformer Mary Carpenter opened the first girls' reformatory in the country in the Red Lodge on Park Row.

14 October 1867   The curtain went up for the first time at the Princes Theatre, Park Row, on a production of Shakespeare's *The Tempest*. The theatre was destroyed during the Bristol Blitz of the Second World War.

17 October 1879   Nearly 1,000 people attended a lecture in Bristol given by Alexander Graham Bell to explain his invention of the telephone.

20 October 1830 The Duchess of Kent and her daughter Princess Victoria stayed at the Mall Hotel, Clifton, during a tour of the West Country.

23 October 1913 Activists campaigning for Votes for Women destroyed by fire a pavilion at Bristol University's sports ground at Coombe Dingle.

25 October 1958 The purpose-built studios of Television Wales and West (TWW) at Arnos Vale, costing £250,000, were opened by the Lord Mayor.

27 October 1818 Church bells rang out as the first cargo from East India arrived at Bristol Docks.

28 October 1904 Chocolatier Joseph Storrs Fry and tobacco baron Henry O. Wills were both granted the Freedom of the City by the Lord Mayor.

3 November 1933 The Archbishop of Canterbury blessed St Mary Redcliffe church at a special service of thanksgiving for the complete restoration of the building.

6 November 1957 Fifteen people on board a Bristol Britannia aircraft were killed when it crashed at Downend on its approach to Filton Airfield, a few miles away.

10 November 1738 The Prince and Princess of Wales visited Bristol for two days, costing the Corporation £954 for their entertainment.

12 November 1851 Charles Dickens appeared at the Victoria Rooms in a farce he had written called *Mr Nightingale's Diary*. He shared the stage with another author, Wilkie Collins.

13 November 1909 Winston Churchill, then President of the Board of Trade, who was in Bristol to address a public meeting, was struck with a dog whip by a suffragette campaigning for Votes for Women.

14 November 1795 Poet Robert Southey married Edith Fricker at St Mary Redcliffe church. The bride was a sister of Samuel Coleridge's wife.

15 November 1899 Queen Victoria opened a convalescent home at Redland without leaving her carriage.

16 November 1910 Three miners were killed and twenty-seven injured in an accident at a colliery in Soundwell.

21 November 1888 Three people perished when a schooner laden with more than 300 barrels of petroleum spirit exploded in Bathurst Basin.

24 November 1940 Around 200 people were killed and another 689 injured in the first major air raid on the city during the Second World War. Churches, as well as cinemas, theatres, schools, homes and shops were destroyed or badly damaged.

29 November 1921 The Duchess of Beaufort opened the Whiteladies Picture House, Clifton. Films were screened at the cinema until 2001 when it closed.

2 December 1986 The Princess Royal, Her Royal Highness Princess Anne, opened a £3 million extension to HTV's studios at Arnos Vale.

5 December 1968 Students started an eleven-day sit-in at Bristol University's administrative headquarters. They were calling for a bigger say in how the university and its students' union were run.

7 December 1613 Robert Redwood, a wealthy citizen, gave his 'lodge near the marsh' to the city for conversion into a public library. It was one of the country's earliest free libraries. The building is now a restaurant.

8 December 1864 Clifton Suspension Bridge was officially opened as a monument to its designer Isambard Kingdom Brunel, who had died five years earlier.

9 December 1878   The West of England and South Wales
                   District Bank in Corn Street closed with
                   large debts after making 'impudent loans'.

13 December 1737   The first inpatients were admitted to Bristol
                   Infirmary. The hospital had been treating
                   outpatients for the previous six months.

15 December 1826   A woman and four children were burnt
                   to death in a house fire in Wine Street.

17 December 1971   Concorde 001, the first pre-production
                   aircraft, made its maiden flight from
                   Filton to Fairford, Gloucestershire.

21 December 2012   Filton Airfield was closed after more than
                   a century of aircraft taking off and landing.
                   The site was sold for redevelopment.

22 December 1878   Fire destroyed St George parish church in
                   east Bristol. It was rebuilt at a cost of £6,000
                   and reopened eighteen months later.

24 December 1958   A Bristol Britannia plane flown by the British
                   Overseas Airways Corporation crashed into the
                   sea near Christchurch, Dorset. Two of the five
                   crew and all seven passengers lost their lives.

25 December 1281   Edward I spent Christmas in Bristol.

26 December 1833   Isambard Kingdom Brunel was appointed
                   chief engineer of the Great Western Railway.

28 December 1654   Oliver Cromwell ordered the
                   destruction of Bristol Castle.

29 December 1976   An early morning gas explosion at the bottom
                   of Park Street ripped apart shops and offices
                   causing damage of around £1 million.

30 December 1945   The first bananas to reach this country
                   after a five-year break during the Second
                   World War arrived at Avonmouth Docks.

ABOUT THE AUTHOR

MAURICE FELLS is a born and bred Bristolian who is passionate about the city's bountiful and rich history. He loves delving into Bristol's archives and reading old newspapers.

He has held key editorial posts in regional newspapers and television and now works as a freelance journalist and author. He is a familiar voice on BBC Radio Bristol, discussing local history matters.

In addition to this book, Maurice has also written *The A-Z of Curious Bristol* and is currently researching and writing *Bristol Plaques*, both published by The History Press.

Also from The History Press

BRISTOL

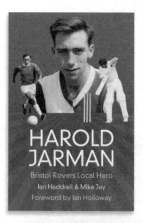

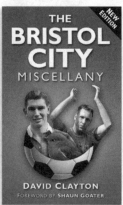

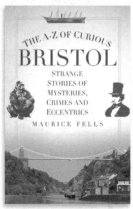

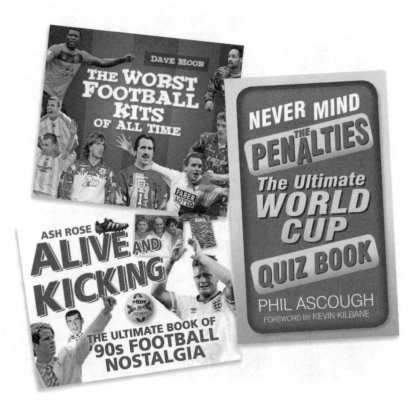

Also from The History Press

FADING ADS

Take a photographic journey into an often overlooked advertising history and see how a region's businesses of old made use of hand-painted signs to inform, advertise and appeal to consumers. Richly illustrated, this series reveals the many varied industries, businesses and companies of yesteryear that now appear faded – like ghosts – on the brickwork of buildings. It is a snapshot of a time that is almost forgotten but which lives on through the sometimes haunting presence of ghost signs on the streets and buildings we walk past.

FADING ADS OF
LONDON
HELEN COX

FADING ADS OF
GLOUCESTER
CHRIS WEST
FOREWORD BY SAM ROBERTS

Also from The History Press

WHEN
DISASTER
STRIKES